Florence, A Delicate Case

The Marble Quilt

In Maremma: Life and a House in Southern Tuscany
(with Mark Mitchell)

Martin Bauman; or, A Sure Thing

The Page Turner

Arkansas

Italian Pleasures (with Mark Mitchell)

While England Sleeps

A Place I've Never Been

Equal Affections

The Lost Language of Cranes

Family Dancing

Florence,
A Delicate Case

David Leavitt

BLOOMSBURY

Published by Bloomsbury, New York and London
Distributed to the trade by Holtzbrinck Publishers

Library of Congress Cataloging-in-Publication Data

Leavitt, David, 1961–
Florence, a delicate case / David Leavitt.
p.cm. – (The writer and the city series ; 3)
ISBN 1-58234-239-3
1. Florence (Italy)–Description and travel. 2. Florence (Italy)–
Social life and customs.
3. Leavitt, David, 1961—Homes and haunts–Italy–Florence.
4. Gay men–Italy–Florence–Biography.
I. Title. II. Writer and the city ; 3

DG734.23 .L43 2002
945'.51–dc21   2001056528

First U.S. Edition 2002

10 9 8 7 6 5 4 3 2 1

Typeset by Hewer Text Ltd, Edinburgh
Printed by Clays Ltd, St Ives plc
Endpaper Map Copyright © 2002 by Jeff Fisher

ACKNOWLEDGEMENTS

For help of many kinds during the researching and writing of this book, I owe a debt of gratitude to Mark Roberts of the British Institute Library, Florence; Liz Calder, architect of this wonderful series; Colin Dickerman and Edward Faulkner at Bloomsbury; Jin Auh, Rose Gaete and Andrew Wylie at the Wylie Agency; James Lord; and most especially Edmund White, whose encouragement and support have mattered more to me over the years than he probably realizes.

This book could be dedicated to no one other than Mark Mitchell, the other half of the 'we' that narrates some of its pages. It was Mark who first brought us to Florence, in 1993; already he knew the city so well that for weeks I failed to learn its geography, so much easier was it just to follow him. He took me to see Benozzo Gozzoli's frescoes at the Palazzo Medici-Riccardi, and the building where Forster had slept. He introduced me to the ex-seminarian from Cosenza who liked to wear baroque liturgical vestments, and compelled me to try tripe. Later on, when I was writing, he brought to my attention all sorts of books I might otherwise not have looked at, read patiently through many drafts, and gave me the benefit of his great editorial skill. I am not exaggerating when I say that without him, this slim volume would never have seen the light of day.

I am nothing if not cultivated; or, at least, the world only expects culture from me. But, in my heart of hearts, I do not believe in culture except as an adjunct to life.

– John Addington Symonds,
in his memoirs

CHAPTER ONE

Florence has always been a popular destination for suicides. In the summer of 1993, when we first moved to the city, a girl jumped to her death from the top of the bell tower next to the Duomo. By the time we walked past, all that was left was a tennis shoe hanging from the scaffolding. *La Nazione*, Florence's newspaper, reported that she had been a foreigner, a tourist, which came as no surprise. A few months before, a vague acquaintance of ours, an actor whose career and marriage were both foundering, had flown in from Los Angeles, checked himself into the Hotel Porta Rossa, and promptly swallowed a bottle of antidepressants. He succeeded only in making him-

David Leavitt

self violently ill, however, and after a few days in the hospital of Santa Maria Nuova, returned to California, to resume his down-at-heel life. In 1953, the American novelist John Horne Burns, author of *The Gallery*, is said to have drunk himself to death at the bar of the Hotel Excelsior. (Ernest Hemingway, one of Burns's admirers, told Robert Manning, 'There was a fellow who wrote a fine book and then a stinking book about a prep school, and then he just blew himself up.') Old-world Florentine hotel rooms seem to be part of the allure, with their high ceilings, their fumaroles of dust, the door keys hanging from brass bells so heavy a pair of them could drag you to the bottom of the Arno.

I exaggerate here – which is easy to do in a city so fond of pomp, of ceremonies and regattas. We have a friend in Florence, a former seminarian (*not* Florentine; he comes from Cosenza, in the South), who every year at *carnevale* dresses in a set of heavily brocaded eighteenth-century liturgical vestments 'borrowed' from a church cabinet to which he, as church organist, has a key. Striding through the streets as if at the head of some

2

religious procession, he exhibits all the *baldanza*, the grandiosity, of Cardinal Richelieu, or the grim reaper. In Florence death seems at once less fearsome and more glamorous than in other places, perhaps thanks to the superabundance of mortified Christs, many of them medieval and grimacing, with raw-looking wounds. On the newly restored cupola of the cathedral of Santa Maria del Fiore (or the Duomo, as it is more commonly known), Vasari's visions of heaven rise above a congested underworld in which unrepentant souls endure gruesome agonies. A long investigation into the case of the 'Monster of Florence', a serial killer who murdered sixteen people between 1968 and 1985, has come to the conclusion that the 'monster' was in the employ of a Satanic cult, the members of which includes some of the city's most powerful citizens, as well as agents of the Italian equivalent of the CIA. No wonder Hannibal Lecter decided to move here!

Of all those who have written about Florence, none caught its weird morbidity better than Walter Pater, who attributed to the Florentines of the fifteenth century 'a practical decision that to be preoccupied with the thought of death was in itself dignifying, and a note of high quality . . . How often, and in what various ways, had they seen life stricken down, in their streets and houses!' It is no coincidence that near the beginning of E.M. Forster's *A Room with a View* (1908), the most famous novel to be set in Florence, a murder is committed in broad daylight, in the Piazza della Signoria, and witnessed by Lucy Honeychurch, who, being English, promptly faints. Blood stains some photographs she has just purchased from Alinari, which George Emerson, having first rescued her, throws into the Arno. Yet the episode draws the pair together, and changes them both. 'For something extraordinary has happened,' George says. 'I must face it without getting muddled. It isn't exactly that a man has died.'

No, not exactly. But then again, what is 'it'? Exactly?

Almost a hundred years after *A Room with a View*, tourists still come to Florence seeking 'it'; and not just 'the barbarian hordes from the North' decried by Mary McCarthy, surging into town on buses from which they are disgorged like so many termites out of an exploded nest; also sober, cautious, well-read, intensely earnest visitors as avid as Lucy Honeychurch to enter 'the real Florence', to penetrate that elusive membrane that separates tourist experience from what might be called – if finding the right words is difficult, it is because the concept is unreal – 'genuine' experience. Such visitors avoid at all costs restaurants with menus printed in English, even though these are often the better restaurants. Determined to steer clear of tourist-trap hotels, they stay in charming, if expensive, bed-and-breakfasts, and would never be seen carrying a phrase book. What they want from Florence is what George wants from Florence, what Pater wanted from Florence, what the young Forster wanted from Florence: that is, to satisfy in Florence some elusive idea of personal fulfillment with which the city's reputation has always been bound up – this despite the fact that so much about Florence promotes a contrary image.

To the contemporary visitor, Florence can seem alternately officious and vulgar, in some quarters brusquely unwelcoming and in others pandering to the lowest tourist impulse. Take a stroll through the Piazza della Signoria on a warm spring morning, and you may think that you have walked into an art historical Disney World, with serpentine lines at the Uffizi and Michelangelo's *David* (the fake one) playing the role of Mickey Mouse. Go 'off the beaten track', however, as Lucy tries to do with the novelist Eleanor Lavish, and as likely as not you will find yourself looking at little else besides stone façades. Many of the streets are so narrow that a normal-sized car passing through will force you up against a wall, like a terrified cat. Everywhere you turn there are doors so immense that smaller, human-sized doors have had to be cut into them; there are even doors the wood of which has been carved to make them resemble stone. All are locked – yet when one of them opens, and an old schnauzer emerges from behind it, yanking at the leash held by his Contessa, for the millisecond that she fiddles with her key, you will catch a glimpse of the fountained courtyard within, scented by lemon and magnolia trees, English dogwood, and thick wisteria vines tendrilling around old ironwork.

Then the door crashes shut, and you are alone
again with what McCarthy called the 'bossy
surfaces' of the façades.

A feeling of exclusion, of pointedly not
being invited to some wonderful party ob-
scurely glimpsed, or perhaps just guessed at,
has always been part of the tourist's experience
of Florence – and not just exclusion from 'the
real Florence' of the Florentines, but from the
rarefied world occupied by expatriates from
the home country. Thus Reverend Eager tries
to seduce Lucy Honeychurch by offering to
introduce her to the residential colony, 'the
people who never walked about with Baede-
kers, who had learned to take a siesta after
lunch, who took drives the pension tourists
had never heard of, and saw by private influence galleries which were closed to them'. As
he confides to Lucy, 'we residents sometimes
pity you poor tourists not a little – handed
about like a parcel of goods from Venice to
Florence, from Florence to Rome, living
herded together in pensions and hotels, quite
unconscious of anything that is outside Bae-
deker, their one anxiety to get "done" or
"through" and go on somewhere else'.

The resident speaks, here and elsewhere, with a sniffy superiority. Yet he or she too, one must remember, was once a tourist; he or she, too, once came to Florence for the first time, bewildered and uncertain and reliant on a guidebook – unless he or she happens to have been born here, like John Singer Sargent or Harold Acton or Florence Nightingale, in which case that experience of virginity is merely displaced by a generation. Do not confuse Florence with a welcoming city; it repulses the new arrival with a hard jab in the side, a frigid stare. Look carefully at the façade of the Duomo, and you will discern, to the right of the right set of doors, an angel making an offensive gesture, right arm crooked, hand balled into a fist, left hand resting on right biceps: *vaffanculo*!

Arriving is rarely easy. The wind at the airport is so strong that flights often have to be diverted to Pisa, and the passengers bused to the city center. Trains pulling in at the station of Santa Maria Novella (a handsome testament to Fascist atavism) egest their human cargo into a confusing mob of commuters, taxi drivers, hotel touts, guides, gypsies, *drageurs*, beggars, and bewildered tourists marooned on suitcase islands. The line for taxis is usually long; to get into town by foot, you walk through an underground corridor lined with discount CD shops, along the edges of which drug addicts huddle with their sedated dogs.

Hotels tend to be expensive, and almost always booked in advance. The visitor who shows up in Florence without a reservation must endure rejection, even embarrassment, as proprietor after proprietor – having first expressed his or her astonishment that the accommodation seeker has not called ahead – refers him on, until he ends up at one of the small hotels or pensions near the station that send out the touts, and that seem always to have rooms available: dank, overpriced rooms that overlook close courtyards or roaring streets. Most of the restaurants are bad, and even the good ones throw up obstacles to their own enjoyment. Cibreo, one of the most famous restaurants in town, is divided into two parts, an expensive *ristorante* and a less expensive *trattoria*, where you get the same food at half the price. At the trattoria, how-

ever, you have to sit on chairs that challenge
the sturdiest back, crowd with strangers at tiny
tables, gasp amid cigarette fumes. The food is
authentically, one might even say rigorously,
Tuscan. Pasta is never served; instead the first
course is usually a bean soup, a reminder that
in other parts of Italy the Tuscans are known
as the *mangiafagioli*: the bean eaters. Offal
features prominently on the menu. The signature *secondo* is *collo di pollo*, stuffed chicken
neck. By the same token, the *centro storico*
abounds with food stands where you can get
sandwiches of tripe or *lampredotto*, which is
the same thing as tripe, only taken from another of the cow's several stomachs. The bread
is unsalted. *La Cucina Fiorentina* privileges
guts, in both senses of the word.

Let me continue my catalogue of the city's
ills, with the proviso that its pleasures will be
sung in a short time. The weather is often
terrible, since Florence occupies the *conca*,
or basin, that spreads out between two important sets of hills – the Mugello to the north
and Chianti to the south. In summer the air
grows sultry, *afoso*; the movie theaters, few of
which, in any case, are air-conditioned, shut

down for the season, as the wealthier Florentines head off to their beach houses in Viareggio, Versilia, and Forte dei Marmi. Winter is no better, with a wind that bears in its icy arms all manner of exotic and undocumented species of flu. And yet for years, Florence was looked upon as an ideal destination for the recovering invalid, praised for its salubrious climate, with the result that many sufferers of tuberculosis moved here in the hopes of recuperating. The cruel trick of those malarial Augusts and penetrating Januarys was certainly not lost upon those who arrived in ill health, got sicker, and died.

One of these was Charles Kenneth Scott Moncrieff, now remembered mostly as the translator of Proust, though he also translated the *Song of Roland* and Stendhal. Like many who emigrated to Florence in the earlier part of the last century, Scott Moncrieff had always been something of an outsider in his native England. At the age of eighteen, he published 'Evensong and Morwe Song' – described by Paul Fussell as 'a bravely obscene story of adolescent fellation' – in the pageant issue of *New Field*, the literary magazine he edited at

Winchester School, which promptly expelled him. Later, he was wounded in the foot on the Western Front, after which he walked with a limp. In London he moved in the same circles as the Uranian poets ('united in their admiration of boys'), made passes at Wilfred Owen, and was the sometime lover of Christopher Millard, Robert Ross's secretary and Oscar Wilde's first bibliographer.

Scott Moncrieff moved to Florence in the nineteen twenties. In *Adventures of a Bookseller*, G. Pino Orioli described him as 'not what I should call a lovable creature; on the contrary, nobody was more prone to take offence. He liked quarrelling on every pretext and with every friend of his, though the quarrels never lasted for long, since he was one of those who cannot live without friends; but for this trait he would have lost them all for good.'

Orioli attributes Scott Moncrieff's ill humor, at least in part, to his foot injury – which did not stop him from taking long walks and even walking tours. 'We sometimes walked about the pine woods at Viareggio,' Orioli recalled, 'where I had an opportunity of seeing how he did his work.'

He carried in his left hand the French volume he was translating, read a few lines of it, interrupted his reading in order to talk to me, and then took a notebook out of his pocket and wrote in English the few lines he had just read, leaning against a pine tree. Then the reading would begin again, then the talk, then the translation into English. He was furious when I told him that I had passed through my Proust stage, and was utterly sick of Swann and that tiresome Albertine.

Scott Moncrieff followed another Anglo-Florentine tradition by converting to Catholicism; indeed, the intensity of his devotion perplexed Orioli, who recalled leaving him alone in the bitter cold of the Duomo in Pisa in the middle of Christmas Mass, 'saying that I had no intention of catching pneumonia. He would not speak to me at all after that. On meeting him later in Florence he began the conversation by telling me that I was a heretic and would go to Hell.'

Orioli's response to this threat illustrates the pay-as-you-go attitude of many Italian Catholics:

A fellow who translates a book about Sodom and Gomorrah written by a Jew deserves to go to Hell and certainly will, unless he repents. As for me, I can't possibly go there, because we have been good Catholics ever since Catholicism has existed, and because we have had an endless number of pious priests in our family, not to mention Cardinal Orioli, my father's grand-uncle. Wait till you have a Cardinal in your family. Then you can begin sending people to Hell.

This *riposte*, as Orioli cheerfully concludes, undid poor Scott Moncrieff, who had to 'cross himself five or six times in order to keep calm'. Yet for the expatriate translator, already in bad health, the afterlife was not merely a subject for banter. In fact, he died not much later, at the age of forty. A poem he had written several years previously, called 'Growing Old Early' (a reply, perhaps, to Matthew Arnold's pessimistic 'Growing Old'), provides an epitaph not only for him but for many of the ailing Englishmen and women who settled in Florence:

Yet now, in Autumn's granary, pent
From splitting frost and scattering wind,
Security in banishment,
   Rest after growth I find.

Rest after growth. Norman Douglas, visiting Scott Moncrieff on his deathbed in 1930, described him as 'shrivelled into a monkey, and not recognisable'. Orioli, who accompanied Douglas on this visit, wrote that he 'held a crucifix and a rosary in his hands, and wore a string of pious medals round his neck'. It was the moment just before 'the colors deepened and grew small' – as Wallace Stevens wrote in another poem, appositely titled 'Anglais Mort à Florence'.

Florence is the only European city I can think of whose most famous citizens, at least for the last hundred and fifty years or so, have all been foreigners. With whom, after all, do we associate this city? Well, Harold Acton to start with, whose Villa La Pietra has recently become the Tuscan campus of New York University. (Better remembered for his conversation than his books, he was the reputed

David Leavitt

model for Anthony Blanche in Evelyn Waugh's
Brideshead Revisited – a 'smear' he spent
much of his later life trying to erase.) Forster
comes to mind, though he spent only five
weeks in Florence as a young man. So does
the great art historian Bernard Berenson. (*His*
villa, I Tatti, on Via Vincigliata, now belongs
to Harvard.) Today, close to twenty-five
American universities maintain campuses in
Florence, with the result that the city teems
with American college students. There is an
American bakery, Carly's, and an American
bar, The Red Garter. Movies are shown in
versione originale with subtitles, still a rarity in
the rest of Italy. In Florence one often meets
American women who came here as students,
fell in love with Florentine men, and married
them. My stepsister, Leslie Blumen, was one of
these. During a semester abroad she met Mar-
cello, with whom she lived for a couple of
years in an apartment on Via delle Belle
Donne. After they married they moved to
Washington, DC, where she opened a shop
selling Florentine paper. More commonly,
American women who marry Florentine
men stay in Tuscany. An example is our

friend Emily Rosner, who now runs, with her husband Maurizio, an American bookshop in Florence, the Paperback Exchange on Via Fiesolana. Their sons, perfectly bilingual, contrast sharply with the offspring of the original Anglo-Florentines, who were usually given over to Tuscan women to be raised. 'Anglo-Becero' these children were called – 'Anglo yokels' – because of the accent they picked up from their minders. By the same token, Florentine aristocrats often hired British nannies to raise their children, who ended up speaking cockney English.

According to Italians, Tuscans speak the purest Italian, if not the most beautiful. (The ideal is *'una lingua Toscana in una bocca Romana'* – a Tuscan tongue in a Roman mouth.) This may be why the city also abounds in language schools, most of them named after great Renaissance figures such as Dante and Michelangelo. Mark and I studied Italian at the British Institute, which Acton founded in the nineteen thirties with his friend the biographer Joan Haslip. Here most of our fellow students were English, many of them teenagers on their way to Oxford or Cambridge. One of the girls, whose parents had a house in Chianti, complained that when she tried to speak Italian to 'the peasants', she could not understand their replies 'because they haven't got any teeth'. What she might actually have been hearing was the famous aspirated 'C' of Florence, which turns the word *casa* (house), for example, into 'hasa'. A drollery in the rest of Italy is to go up to a Florentine in a bar and ask him to order 'a Coca-Cola with a short straw'. (*Una Hoha-Hola h*on *un h*annuccia *h*orta.)

As the saying goes, however, the best place to learn a language is in bed, and so most of the American women we know in Florence speak flawless Tuscan Italian, right down to the aspirated 'C'. Many live in rambling apartments, or farmhouses high in the hills, twenty minutes outside of town – a far cry from the pensions where they sojourned in student days. These pensions still thrive, though, and every year, more students arrive, tides of them, some of whom end up staying for the rest of their lives. They lend the city an atmosphere not unlike that of an American university town. Because of them, perhaps, pizza is immensely popular here, though as a dish the pizza has its origins in Naples. One afternoon at Yellow Bar, an immense pizzeria on Via del Proconsolo, we ended up sharing a table with an American woman in her forties and a Roman man in his seventies. It turned out that she was the design director for Ferragamo and that he had opened the first-ever pizzeria in Florence, some twenty-five years earlier. Such a grouping is fairly easy to fall into here, and if I report it with some surprise, it is only because it took place not at the chic Trattoria delle Belle Donne, or at Cibreo, but at Yellow Bar with its Buffalo Bill posters, its menu in English, and its crew of touts sent out into the center every afternoon to hand out flyers: in short, at the very sort of 'tourist' restaurant that as a student visiting Florence in the early nineteen eighties I would have avoided like the plague. Yet it was also at Yellow Bar that we once saw Franz Brüggen, conductor of the Orchestra of the Eighteenth Century, having a pizza after a concert at the Teatro della Pergola; at Yellow Bar that we have often seen the earthily handsome Romeo brothers, owners of an office-supply shop on Via della

Condotta, whose penetrating eyes have provoked more than one art historian to spend
twenty minutes choosing a pencil; at Yellow
Bar, finally, that we sometimes see – still handsome after all these years, with thick, graying
hair – the actor who played the carriage driver
in the Merchant-Ivory film of *A Room with a
View*, the one who sends Lucy into the violets
to be kissed by George Emerson. Phaethon – as
Forster called this driver – now runs a souvenir
shop at the top of Via del Proconsolo. He is a
regular at Yellow Bar, usually sitting at a corner
booth, and often accompanied by a beautiful
Japanese woman who may or may not have
come to Italy to seduce him, after seeing her
destiny spelled out one winter afternoon on the
screen of an Osaka cinema, into which she had
run to escape the rain . . . No, probably not.
And yet something about Florence encourages
one to the most sentimental speculation and
fantasy.

In no sense of the word is Florence a 'big' city,
and this has always been part of its appeal. In
Rome you depend on buses, in Paris the *Métro*
and taxis. In Florence, on the other hand, you

can get pretty much anywhere you need to on foot, even the countryside, which opens out just beyond the Belvedere, at the top of Costa San Giorgio. Or perhaps I should say, you can get everywhere you need to on foot if you begin your trek within the limits of what Henry James called 'the compact and belted mass of which the Piazza della Signoria [is] the immemorial centre'. Writing in 1873, James was already lamenting the 'expansion' of this mass, 'under the treatment of enterprising syndics, into an ungirdled organism of the type, as they viciously say, of Chicago; one of those places of which, as their grace of a circumference is nowhere, the dignity of a centre can no longer be predicated'.

It would not please James to learn that a hundred and thirty years later, the expansion has only intensified, its most recent efflorescence being the construction of a tram to connect the city center with the suburb of Scandicci, where the novelist Ouida once lived, and which is now a glut of ugly apartment buildings. Such a tram the sophisticated tourist would be unlikely to take; as a rule he moves in more wholesome directions, out into Chianti, for example, or up to Fiesole or Settignano, where Michelangelo grew up. For the tourist, despite all his claims to want to see the 'real Florence', isn't interested in its urban sprawl; he is interested in what Bernard Berenson called 'conoscing', the object of which is the discovery of unsuspected marvels. (The term derives from the Italian verb *conoscere*, 'to know'.) He wants to bring home, if not photographic evidence, then at least the interior knowledge that he has partaken of all the marvels that Florence has to offer – as if that were possible in the course of a single human life.

And what marvels there are! Astonishingly, Florence houses almost a fifth of the world's art treasures. A fifth! A thorough Florentine itinerary takes in architecture, sculpture and painting, major museums (The Bargello and the Uffizi) as well as small ones (the Stibbert and the Horne), public buildings, palaces and innumerable churches, Botticellis and Leonardos and Michelangelos and Giottos and Masaccios and Beato Angelicos and Gozzolis and Pontormos and Donatellos . . . And even if you see all of these things, even if you stay in

Florence a year, or five years, there will still be something that you've missed, some remote church known only to the cognoscenti of *conoscing*, about which you will be informed only on the eve of your departure.

Nineteenth-century travelers, who usually visited Florence for a month or even several months, were able to take things at a slower pace, to intersperse their art wanderings with tea and shopping and social calls. (William Dean Howells's 1886 novel *Indian Summer* describes just such a Florentine 'season'.) When Clara Schumann came to Florence in 1880, her hostess, Lisl von Herzogenberg, wrote to Brahms that in order to appreciate the city fully, more time would be required 'than her round-ticket – awful invention – permits her . . .' And yet her reaction to what she did see suggests that Madame Schumann might have been grateful for the round-trip ticket.

It has happened a couple of times that we found her sitting on her stool before a Signorelli or a Verrocchio looking very worried, rubbing her hands in fearful enthusiasm – she would not let

herself be emotionally carried away or allow her
soul, so capable of vibration, to stir.

Soon, of course, the round-trip ticket would
give way to even more awful inventions, such
as the commercial airliner; as travel became
easier, the length of the average visit to Florence would shrink, so that today the habit is to
see the city in a few days or even a few hours.
The result is an even more intense version of
the sensory overload that Madame Schumann
suffered. By 1989, Graziella Magherini, a psy-
chiatrist working at the Santa Maria Nuova
hospital, had observed so many cases of foreigners quite literally collapsing from too
much art that she labelled the phenomenon
'Stendhal's Syndrome', after an episode in the
novelist's diary in which he recalled suffering
palpitations and a falling sensation during a
visit to the basilica of Santa Croce in 1817.
'*J'étais déjà dans une sorte d'extase,*' Stendhal
wrote, '*par l'idée d'être à Florence, et le voi-
sinage des grands hommes dont je venais de
voir les tombeaux. Absorbé dans la contem-
plation de la beauté sublime, je la voyais de
près, je la touchais pour ainsi dire. J'étais*

arrivé a ce point d'émotion où se rencontrent les sensations célestes données par les beaux-arts et les sentiments passionnés. En sortant de Santa Croce, j'avais un battement de coeur . . .; la vie était épuisée chez moi, je marchais avec la crainte de tomber.'

It's easy to understand how he felt. Especially for those of us inured to more banal provinces, the immanence of the old, the beautiful and the historic in almost every facet of quotidian life takes some getting used to. For example, when Mark and I first moved to Florence in the early nineteen nineties, we rented an apartment in a *palazzo* on Via dei Neri with a statue of Mercury in its foyer; a plaque posted on the façade of this building announced that here, in 1594, Ottavio Rinuccini – 'letterato illustre e gentile poeta' – had written *La Dafne*, a 'pastoral fable' that Jacopo Corsi and Jacopo Peri would soon transform into the world's first opera. Under such circumstances, reality can start to seem like a guidebook, just as a terrace view that includes, among innumerable rooftops and green copper domes, the church of San Miniato al Monte, the *Belvedere*, and the hills of Chianti

David Leavitt

across the river, can start to seem like a postcard. It ceases to mean anything to you – or
perhaps I should say that *you* cease to mean
anything to *it*. Such views, we say, awe, they
overwhelm ... Every verb connected with
Florentine views implies collapse, submission.
There are moments, especially in the evening,
when a walk through the Piazza della Signoria
leaves me stunned; more often, however, when
I walk through the piazza, I barely see the
piazza, so focused am I on my own thoughts,
or on the conversation I'm having, or on
weaving a path among the many tour groups
that crowd that part of the city in the spring,
each moving with the singlemindedness of a
school of fish, a flock of migrating birds, and
led by a guide carrying a stick tied with a
gaudy scarf to distinguish herself from all
the other guides. On such occasions, I envy
any newcomer his or her first glimpse of the
piazza, especially if that glimpse takes place
early in the morning, when the place is pretty
much empty except for the pair of dozing
carabiniere who, since the bombing at the
Uffizi almost a decade ago, spend the night
in their car by the Loggia dei Lanzi.

If the best time to look at the piazza is early, just after dawn, the best way to get there is from the river: you walk up the Lungarno Archibusieri, turn right, and suddenly, at the end of the long Uffizi corridor, opening like a pair of forceps, there it is: there you are. You stand, humbled, at the center of the world. The piazza looks you over. Like the Pensione Simi (where Forster first stayed in 1901), it has its permanent residents. Near the Palazzo Vecchio, Neptune soaks in a fountain that is as often as not turned off. The imitation *David* broods, eros dripping from his long fingers. Hercules hammers at the defeated Cacus. Few places in the world are so fraught with historical events. After all, in this piazza, Savonarola burned the vanities, and was burned himself. (A medallion embedded in the pavement marks the spot.) Cellini unveiled his bronze *Perseus*. Michelangelo's *David* was erected, and then, a few hundred years later, moved to the Accademia, along a makeshift length of railroad track. Queen Victoria rode in a carriage through this piazza. Riots took place here, blood was spilled in quantity, and on the balcony of the Palazzo Vecchio, in 1938,

Hitler shook Mussolini's hand while Black-shirts chanted.

Today green algae coats Neptune's calves. The algae is history's athlete's foot. The piazza is the shower room of the ages, where gods and heroes parade naked, display outsize genitals, boast of conquests, show off trophies. It is not a place for women. What women lurk among the statuary do so as wraiths of male hysteria or desire. Polyxena and the Sabines, being raped, calcify sexual bragging. Judith, grappling Holofernes to slice off his head, calcifies sexual terror. Like the advice of mothers, a row of Virtues shrinks to the shadows of the loggia, ignored. A herm, half human, half tree, is the piazza's pin-up girl. Her black fig leaf pulls all attentions toward it like a vanishing point, her flight from lust inciting what it seeks to repel.

At night the impression is even stronger. Torches along the zippered edges of the Palazzo Vecchio lend a glowing radiance to the stones, as if light has made them molten. At this hour the sight of Neptune, the slick white wetness of him, is enough to set the mouth watering. Looking at him, you finally understand why sculptors fought over blocks of white Carrara marble. You want to take off your shoes, wade through the fountain, scrape at the green algae on his flanks with your nails.

CHAPTER TWO

The promise of a destiny, verging on the erotic on one side and the artistic on the other, seems always to have attached itself to Florence in the imagination of the foreigner, drawing him to the city not merely so that he can *see* but so that he can *be* or *become* something more than he is. Or perhaps it would be more accurate to say that in Florence he hopes to retrieve a quality endemic to himself the expression of which the atmosphere of home has stifled. As Pater wrote of the great German art historian Johann Joachim Winckelmann, 'In the fantastic plans of foreign travel continually passing through his mind . . . there seems always to be rather a wistful sense of something lost to be

regained, than the desire of discovering anything new.'

My use of 'he' in the above paragraph, by
the way, is deliberate: *he* is not meant, in this
case, to mean 'he or she' (or 'he and she')
since, historically, men and women seem to
have come to Florence seeking different
things, and when they have left (if they have
left) to have taken different things away. Consider the Lawrences, David and Frieda, so-
journing here just after the Great War.
Describing the Piazza della Signoria in his
1922 novel *Aaron's Rod*, Lawrence's hero
observes that it is 'packed with men: but
all, all men . . . but Men! Men! A town of
men, in spite of everything.' He offers a Whit-
manesque hymn to the *David*, 'white and
stripped in the wet, white against the dark,
warm-dark cliff of the building – and near, the
heavy naked men of Bandinelli . . .'

As might be expected, Frieda had a different
take on things; while concurring with her
husband that Florence was 'a men's town'
(Mary McCarthy called it 'a manly town'),
she also complained that it struck her 'as being
like [Mrs Gaskell's novel] "Cranford", only it

was a man's "Cranford". And the wickedness there seemed like old maids' secret rejoicing in wickedness. Corruption is not interesting to me, nor does it frighten me. I find it dull.'

That dullness, which persists to this day, is the antonym of Paterian longing, and often leads to vitriol and complaint, particularly at those expatriate dinner parties at which no Italian accent is heard, and the topic of conversation is inevitably Italian inefficiency, Italian bureaucracy, Italian inflexibility . . . all of which, up to a point, is understandable, given that the negotiation of a culture as elaborate and tradition-bound as Italy's can be frustrating, and one derives natural comfort from the commiseration of a countryman. And yet at these dinners there often comes a moment when I want to throw up my hands and say, 'Well, if you hate it here so much, why don't you leave?'

It was the same toward the end of the nineteenth century, when Florence had a reputation (broadcast by its English residents) for being, in Walter Savage Landor's words, 'the filthiest capital in Europe'. Nazar Litrov, a Russian manservant who accompanied

David Leavitt

Tchaikovsky to Florence in 1890, noted in his diary that 'at almost every building one can urinate on the streets without any ceremony, ladies and girls don't pay any attention . . .' Litrov's tone is refreshingly unjudgmental; on the other hand, the English painter William Holman Hunt expressed both disgust and affront at the city's 'stinks':

What do you think of a boy of fifteen or sixteen in the blazing sunlight at one o'clock on Sunday, in Kensington Gore say, taking his breeches down for a necessary purpose which he performs while he still goes on with his game of pitch and toss with seven or eight companions some two years older who remain in a circle about two or three yards round him. Then again to an old gentleman of the utmost respectability . . . walking across the road at the Duke of York's column and taking down his black cloth breeches for the same purpose.

The rhetorical flourish of relocating the offending scene to the home country begs the question of why Holman Hunt and thirty-thousand other Englishmen were living in

34

Florence in the first place. Also (the homosexual writer feels dutybound to note), when boys took down their breeches in the street, whether in the Piazza della Signoria or Kensington Gore, it was usually for a purpose quite different from the one that Holman Hunt ascribes. Florentine laxities had to have suited the English in some fundamental way, or they would never have gone there in such vast numbers.

Without doubt, the most hectoring and jingoistic English voice at the end of the nineteenth century was that of John Ruskin, for whom the establishment of an omnibus stand at the foot of the bell tower provided an excuse to rant against what he saw as Florence's poor stewardship of its art treasures. Among many other things, Ruskin lamented that 'the hackney coaches, with their more or less farmyard-like litter of occasional hay, and smell of variously mixed horse manure,' made it 'impossible to stand for a moment near the Campanile . . . not a soul in Florence ever caring for the sight of any piece of its old artists' work'. It was probably of Ruskin that the young Henry James was thinking when in

the 1870s he addressed 'the so terribly actual
Florentine question . . . a battle-ground, today, in many journals, with all Italy practically
pulling on one side and all England, America
and Germany pulling on the other . . .'

The little treasure-city is, if there ever was one, a
delicate case – more delicate perhaps than any
other in the world save that of our taking on
ourselves to persuade the Italians that they
mayn't do as they like with their own. They
so absolutely may that I see no happy issue from
the fight. It will take more tact than our combined tactful genius may at all probably muster
to convince them that their own is, by an ingenious logic, much rather *ours*.

While James agreed with Ruskin that 'A cab-
stand is a very ugly and dirty thing, and
Giotto's Tower should have nothing in common with such conveniences,' he considered
that 'discord for discord, there isn't much to
choose between the importunity of the
author's personal ill-humour and the incon-
gruity of horse-pails and bundles of hay'.
    What most troubled James about Ruskin's

'insidious and insane' tract, however, was its preoccupation with the idea of error. 'A truce to all rigidities is the law of the place,' he noted in a Paterian moment. 'Differences here are not iniquity and righteousness; they are simply variations of temperament, kinds of curiosity.' For James, Ruskin is a kind of priggish deacon or schoolmaster, a forerunner of Forster's Reverend Eager, leading his flock on a theological/art historical tour of the city. 'Nothing in fact is more comical,' James observed, 'than the familiar asperity of the author's style and the pedagogic fashion in which he pushes and pulls his unhappy pupils about, jerking their heads toward this, rapping their knuckles for that, sending them to stand in corners and giving them Scripture texts to copy.'

This is Reverend Eager to a tee: what he wants to teach his parishioners is 'how to worship Giotto, not by tactile valuations, but by the standards of the spirit'. For Reverend Eager, the significance of Santa Croce lies not in its inherent beauty, nor in its status as the 'pantheon' of Florence's illustrious dead (Machiavelli, Michelangelo, Rossini), but in the fact that it was 'built by faith in the full fervour of medievalism, before any taint of the Renaissance had appeared'. In this regard he typifies the English tendency to extol what Pater called the 'rude strength' of the Middle Ages at the expense of corrupting Renaissance innovations. Aesthetics, for Forster, encode politics, and behind Reverend Eager's tedious encomia to Giotto one hears the parliamentarian Henry Labouchère decrying the 'insufficiency of the severest sentence that the law allows' in the case of Oscar Wilde. One also hears the critics and curates who attacked Pater's *The Renaissance* on its publication, accusing its author of immorality and antireligiosity, of leading 'minds weaker than [his] own' into the cave of error. Even as fine a mind as George Eliot dismissed the book as 'quite poisonous in its false principles of criticism and false conception of life', and Pater, in a gesture of cowardly back-pedalling, removed the famous 'Conclusion' from the second edition, restoring it only in 1888. (He had been concerned, he wrote, that 'it might possibly mislead some of those young men into whose hands it might fall. On the whole, I have thought it best to reprint it here, with some slight changes which bring it closer to my original meaning.')

The danger of *The Renaissance*, in the view of its critics, lay in Pater's advocacy of sensory experience, which was seen by the Reverend John Wordsworth, among others, as suggesting 'that no fixed principles either of religion or morality can be regarded as certain, that the only thing worth living for is momentary enjoyment and that probably or certainly the soul dissolves at death into elements which are destined never to reunite'. In fact, Pater had little interest in the afterlife; his primary concern was with apprehension itself, as evidenced by the credo: 'Not the fruit of experience, but experience itself, is the end.' By contrast, progress, expansion and Empire were the watchwords of the Victorians, of whom he might have been speaking when he noted that in the Middle Ages, 'the crushing of the sensuous, the shutting of the door upon it, the ascetic interest, is already traceable'.

It was against the Victorian creed of self-discipline and self-denial that Pater, knowingly or otherwise, waged battle in *The Renaissance*, not directly, but rather by exalting its opposite: 'any stirring of the senses, strange dyes, strange colours, and curious odours, or work of the artist's hands, or the face of one's friend'. He writes approvingly of play, 'the unexpected blessedness of what may seem our least important part of time; not merely because play is in many instances that to which people really apply their own best powers, but also because at such times, the stress of our servile, everyday attentiveness being relaxed, the happier powers in things without us are permitted free passage, and have their way with us'.

Nor does Pater shrink, as this passage indicates, from explicitly erotic language, even if he eschews, in *The Renaissance*, any direct mention of sex. Instead language does the job, so that when, in his most famous phrase, he describes success in life as 'to burn with this hard, gemlike flame, to maintain this ecstasy', he ends up giving voice to the more explicit frustrations that we have come to look at as definitive of his epoch. A brazen age is impatient for spectacular gestures, but in those years the mere evocation of David and

Jonathan or 'the Greeks' – even the utterance of the word 'Hellenic' – awakened the possibility of a life free from the punitive rigidities of Victorianism. As a result, the term 'aesthetic' began to be looked upon as having lewd or improper connotations. By 1903, Rollo St Clair Talboys, tutor to Ronald Firbank, was worrying lest his young charge should fall prey to 'the cult of the purple orchid' and become 'a Parisian mondain of the de Goncourt school . . . a slave of the senses – an emotional bon vivant to the last tremolo'. Firbank did, and worse: in his later writing we see Pater's ideas not so much in full flower as at that stage when the petals are beginning to brown, and the heady apricot scent has given way to something mulchy and rotten-sweet.

More about Firbank later. For now, let us consider another English writer who settled in Florence, the novelist Louisa Ramé, better known as Ouida.

Born in 1839 in the village of Bury St Edmunds to a French father and an English mother, Ouida started writing early on, taking as a *nom de plume* a childhood

David Leavitt

mispronunciation of her own name. Profit and popularity came swiftly for her, thanks in part to the velocity with which she churned out her turgid, semi-literary novels, which had titles like *Granville de Vigne, Idalia, Pascarel, In Maremma, Two Little Wooden Shoes* and *A Dog of Flanders* (she adored dogs). Neither beautiful nor elegant, Ouida enjoyed, none-theless, an expensive and extravagant life, ordering most of her clothes from Worth and giving parties in her suite at the Langham Hotel in London. She considered herself daring; at these parties, a sign was sometimes posted that read 'Morals and Umbrellas to be Left at the Door'. In the early 1870s – in part, at least, because she was suffering from bronchitis – she moved with her mother to Florence, renting the Villa Farinola in Scandicci (today she could take the tram into town) and throwing herself full force into the social life of the Anglo-Florentine colony, which was then about thirty years old. Although English writers had been traveling to Florence for centuries – among them John Evelyn, Milton, Boswell, Byron, and the Shelleys – the community had only really become entrenched in the 1840s, when Fanny Trollope had established the first Anglo-Florentine dynasty (and literary salon) at the Villino Trollope on the Piazza Maria Antonia (now the Piazza dell'Indipendenza). Her son Thomas carried on the tradition, first at the Villino, then at the Villa Ricorboli, beyond the Porta San Niccolò. Presently the Brownings showed up, settling at Casa Guidi near the Pitti Palace; by this time Florence had started to be known as a refuge for expatriate intellectuals. '*Ville toute Anglaise*,' the Goncourt brothers, Jules and Edmond, declared of the city in 1855, 'where the palaces are almost the same dismal black as the city of London, and where everything seems to smile upon the English . . .' By the time Ouida got there (she was thirty-two), thirty thousand of the two hundred thousand residents of Florence were English or American.

Ouida seems now to have decided to make it one of her Florentine priorities to fall in love. As a suitor, she chose the Marchese della Stufa, who lived not far from her in Scandicci, in a house called Castagnolo. The unmarried Marchese was a scion of the old Florentine aristocracy, a gentleman-in-waiting to King Umberto and a landowner who treated both his agricultural and social duties with the utmost gravity. A few years earlier, in the company of an Englishman named Dr Clement, he had traveled to Burma to investigate the possibility of building a railroad from Mandalay to Rangoon, but nothing had come of the project, and he had returned to Florence, where he now took to escorting not only Ouida but the woman who would become her rival, Janet Ross.

Much has been written, over the years, about Janet Ross, and from what I have read of it, I have developed an intense dislike for the woman. No doubt she was both shrewder and more intelligent than Ouida, yet she hated dogs, and appears to have cultivated with alacrity her own reputation for being 'formidable'. Even her daughter, Lina Waterfield, and her granddaughter, Kinta Beevor – both of whom wrote memoirs of Anglo-Florentine life – seem to have found her intimidating and mean. Herself the author of numerous books, among them *Old Florence and Modern Tuscany* and the 1899 *Leaves from Our Tuscan*

Kitchen (one of the first Italian cookbooks ever published in England and – if the instructions to cook spaghetti 'for nearly twenty minutes' are to be taken as an example – very much geared to Victorian tastes; either that, or pasta was a lot thicker in those days), Mrs Ross held court first at Castagnolo, which she rented from the Marchese, then at Poggio Gherardo, near Settignano, one of the villas in which the storytellers gather in Boccaccio's *Decameron*. Here she distilled a famous vermouth according to a secret recipe that she claimed to have been given by the last of the Medicis, and sold it at the Army and Navy stores in London. Her husband, Henry Ross, was a banker, but she appears to have had little to do with him, and for social purposes, at least, to have sought out the company of her landlord. Then as now, women in the colony whose husbands did not like to go out much had to content themselves with homosexual 'walkers' – a version of the Florentine *cicisbeo* – and this was in all probability the kind of relationship that Mrs Ross enjoyed with the Marchese when Ouida decided to thrust herself into the picture.

Poor Ouida! She simply didn't get it. Although she considered herself forward-thinking, even naughty, in comparison to the Anglo-Florentines she was a *naïf*. When the Marchese refused her demand that he give up his friendship with Mrs Ross as proof of his loyalty to her, she took it for granted that the two were having an affair, and as an act of vendetta, quickly dispatched *Friendship*, a rubbishy roman-à-clef in which she cast the Marchese as the dashing Prince Ioris, herself as the tubercular ingénue Etoile, and Mrs Ross as the shrewish *mondaine* Lady Joan Challoner, who blackmails the good-natured prince in order to guarantee his fidelity. To avoid a libel suit, Ouida also cast Rome as Florence, with the flat *campagna* doing a particularly bad job of interpreting the countryside around Scandicci.

Mrs Ross was outraged. Soon rumor had her attempting to horsewhip Ouida on Via Tornabuoni, and Ouida shooting at Mrs Ross in her villa. All of this is nonsense; what is certain is that Mrs Ross nursed an intractable grudge about the affair, and was said still to be keeping a copy of *Friendship* in her bathroom for use as toilet paper even years after Ouida had died in Viareggio, destitute and forgotten, having starved herself to feed her many dogs.

Ouida is typical of the sort of mediocrity that Florence has latterly attracted. Better writers (Forster, James) came early and left, or came after they were already famous (Browning, Landor). Although Aldous Huxley loved Florence at first, his enthusiasm palled quickly, leading him to move his family to Rome. (In a letter to his brother he wrote, 'After a third-rate provincial town, colonized by English sodomites and middle-aged Lesbians, which is, after all, what Florence is, a genuine metropolis will be lively.') In his Italian diaries, Goethe virtually ignores Florence, noting only that:

I took a quick walk through the city to see the Duomo and the Battistero. Once more, a completely new world opened up before me, but I did not wish to stay long. The location of the Boboli Gardens is marvellous. I hurried out of the city as quickly as I entered it.

David Leavitt

Although Goethe never specifies what drove him to leave so precipitously, a palpable air of unease hangs over this paragraph. Nor is he the only writer whose descriptive capacities the city's darker aspect has managed to flummox. Even James was left at a loss for words, attributing to Florence 'a kind of grave radiance – a harmony of high tints – which I scarce know how to describe'. Many years later Firbank called Florence 'a rather sinister city', and through the voice of Countess Yvorra in *The Flower Beneath the Foot*, implicitly lampooned the river view for which Lucy Honeychurch hearkens:

Ah, and Florence, too, I regret to say I found very far from what it ought to have been!!! I had a window giving onto the Arno, and so I could *observe* . . . I used to see some curious sights! I would not care to scathe your ears, my Innocent, by an inventory of one half of the wantonness that went on; enough to say the tone of the place forced me to fly to Rome, where beneath the shadow of dear St Peter's I grew gradually less distressed.

This last line may also be a gentle elbowing of *A Room with a View*, since in the novel Charlotte Bartlett, to save Lucy from the predatory influences of George Emerson, absconds with the girl to Rome. In both books, Rome – that capital in which Catholic piety shares such an uneasy bed with Pagan splendor – offers itself as an antidote to Florentine dissolution, a place to recuperate and seek absolution. Yet the medicine works in neither case, and in Forster's words, 'the companion who is merely uncongenial in the medieval world becomes exasperating in the classical'. Florence, with its dark alleys, its death worship and sexual secrets, wins out not just for Lucy, but for Isabel Archer, whose Tuscan seduction leads only to the bankrupt Roman marriage that is at the heart of *The Portrait of a Lady*.

As for the writers who stayed in Florence, they wrote mostly about Florence, and themselves: literary travel guides, art history, history, *romans-à-clef*, and of course endless memoirs. Garden know-how combined with gossip is the classic recipe for the Anglo-Florentine memoir, which usually devolves, at some point, into a catalogue of the famous, glimpsed and chatted with. Thus Acton writes in *Memoirs of an Aesthete*:

> In Florence there was a plethora of writers, and you were bound to meet them in the Via Tornabuoni; D.H. Lawrence with his Rubens *frau* and his string bag after marketing; Norman Douglas chewing the cud of a *Toscano*; Ronald Firbank capering into a flower-shop; Aldous Huxley who maintained that in Florence 'every prospect pleases, but only man is vile'; Scott Moncrieff, who kept up a doggerel offensive against the Sitwells in *The New Witness*: dining at Betti's, scandal-mongering in Orioli's bookshop, drinking vermouth at Casone's, there was no avoiding one of these in the city . . .

Acton's prose is at once listless and list-y, as arid as the world it seeks to portray. If he was the scribe of Florence in the nineteen twenties, he was also its avatar, promoting across the channel an image of the city as a Shelleyesque 'paradise of exiles'. Thus when the young Evelyn Waugh (Acton's boyfriend at Oxford) was offered the chance to become Scott Moncrieff's secretary, he lapsed into a reverie in which he was 'drinking Chianti under olive trees and listening to discussions of all the most iniquitous outcasts of Europe'. (In the event, the job fell through.) Likewise the young Jocelyn Brooke, in a memoir of 'Miss Wimpole' published in *Private View* (1954), described a colony synonymous, at least for those back in England, with impropriety:

> Dark hints would be dropped in undertones: Mrs. So-and-so, it seemed, had met Mr Watkins in Florence, and it was *said* . . . Oh yes, it was common talk among the English colony . . . Why, the wretched woman had actually *admitted* it, quite openly . . . And that poor Miss Shute – so talented – one feels quite sorry for her . . . Oh no, no doubt at all – Mrs Bellingham actually *saw* her, coming out of the Red Lion . . . Such a pity – but of course, after that, one can hardly have her to the house, can one?

The reality was rather more tepid. Although there were feuds galore, they were usually more on the level of petty squabbling than

David Leavitt

Shakespearean drama. (An example is Vernon
Lee's long feud with Berenson, after he accused
her of plagiarism.) The Bohemianism of the
Anglo-Florentines, moreover, was of a distinctly neutered variety. In England they had
lived under the threat of social ostracism or
even arrest and imprisonment. In Italy they
were freed from this threat, yet rather than
exult in their liberty, they created for themselves a society as artificial as the 'miniature
castle' that Lord Richard Vermont builds in
Osbert Sitwell's poem 'Milordo Inglese', complete with 'miniature' palace intrigues. (We
will return to Sitwell's poems later. For the
moment, suffice it to say that an odor of frantic
exhaustion clings to them – of children resist-
ing the dusk that will cut off their games.)

In the end, it was less iniquity than spiteful-
ness that distinguished the community. Reviewing *Friendship* in *The Atlantic Monthly*, Harriet
Waters Preston complained of the colony's
'frivolity and irresponsibility, its meanness,
moral and pecuniary, its prostrate subservience
to rank, and its pest of parasitic toadies and
busybodies . . .' Eccentricity itself grew weari-
some. 'There was a Marchese Fioravanti, a

passionate anglophile who gave parties at which guests danced Scottish reels,' writes Caroline Moorehead in her fine biography of the writer Iris Origo. The Marchese also kept a pet crocodile in a pond, 'netted over so that it could not escape, and carried down to the cellar on a stretcher by four men when it showed signs of wanting to hibernate'. When the crocodile died, the Marchese 'had a proper funeral held in its honour, and forever after suspected his mother of its murder'.

John Singer Sargent, though born in Florence, told Acton that he could not paint there. 'The creative artist striving for self-expression must end by feeling oppressed by so much beauty,' wrote Acton (who knew), 'weighed down, like Atlas, with the whole world of art on his shoulders. Where taste is uniformly exquisite, where one is surrounded by masterpieces, one loses initiative in a cloud of wonder. All one's efforts appear to be dwarfed. One asks oneself: what's the use?'

On the other hand, in such an atmosphere the amateur flourishes; as Acton observed of his parents' generation, 'they wrote, they painted, they composed, they collected . . .'

When Mary McCarthy came to Florence in the late 1950s, she showed little patience for the city's foreign colony, on which she blamed the dissemination of a 'false idea of Florence . . . a tooled-leather idea of Florence as a dear bit of the old world. Old maids of both sexes – retired librarians, governesses, ladies with reduced incomes, gentlemen painters, gentlemen sculptors, gentlemen poets, anaemic amateurs and dabblers of every kind – "fell in love" with Florence and settled down to make it home.'

For McCarthy, Colonel G. F. Young, self-appointed defender of the Medicis and author of 'a spluttering "classic" that went through many editions, arguing that the Medicis had been misrepresented by democratic historians', was typical of the Anglo-American visitors who 'expropriated Florence, occupying villas in Fiesole or Bellosguardo, studying Tuscan wild flowers, collecting ghost stories, collecting triptychs and diptychs, burying their dogs in the churchyard of the Protestant Episcopal church, knowing (for the most part) no Florentines but their servants'.

No wonder the art historian John Pope-

Hennessy, in later years, complained of her 'astringent typewriter'! Her take on the Anglo-Florentines is typical of the unmitigated harshness that characterizes *The Stones of Florence*; if Acton, in *Memoirs of an Aesthete*, is the consummate insider, then McCarthy is the consummate outsider, determined to lay claim to the city by laying siege to it. And yet, if the overall effect of her book is to leave the reader feeling that she didn't much like the town she had taken as her subject, this may have been – as her biographer, Frances Kiernan, points out – because, overall, the town didn't much like her. Berenson teased her, while her guide, Roberto Papi, failed to be the *cavaliere servente* she hoped for. As Cristina Rucellai told Kiernan, 'she cannot be positive because her experience was not positive'. *The Stones of Florence*, for all its flashes of charm and intelligence, is finally the *cri de coeur* of yet another tourist who felt shut out.

That said, a touch of insecure American bluster may be just what it takes to cut through decades of cant, and we must be thankful to McCarthy for having the guts to call the foreign colony's notion of Florence 'bookish, synthetic, gushing, insular, genteel, and, above all, proprietary'. When she complains of the 'sickly love' that propels foreign residents to speak of 'our Florence' or 'my Florence', she echoes James in his diatribe against Ruskin a century before. Whatever Florence is, McCarthy argues, it is not 'a dear bit of the Old World. Florence can never have been that, at any time in its existence.'

One can imagine what her reaction would have been to the English gardens that were such a source of pride to the original Anglo-Florentines, in which, as Moorehead notes, olives and vineyards 'were replaced with lawns and deciduous shade trees, herbaceous borders were planted with irises, crocuses, peonies and daffodils, woods and scrub were cleared, and steep dry-stone-walled terraces were covered with roses: Banksias, "Irene Watts" and "Madame Metral"'.

According to James Lord, when Harold Acton's father, Arthur, bought Villa La Pietra (named for a stone pillar indicating a distance of one mile from the old city gate), the first task he undertook was the restoration of the gardens, which had been Anglicized in the nineteenth century. Like Edith Wharton (who coined the phrase), Acton Senior disdained 'flower-loveliness', preferring gardens that re-interpreted the Renaissance tradition. The Italian Renaissance garden was a narrative, the elements of which – fountains, hedges and statuary – worked together to elaborate a theme: the Villa d'Este in Tivoli, for example, described the labors of Hercules, while the Villa Lante at Bagnaia, built for Cardinal Gambara, Bishop of Viterbo, made a play on the similarity of his name to the word for crayfish (*gambero*) by incorporating cray-fish motifs into its design. *Giochi d'acqua* – secret squirting fountains that doused the legs of unsuspecting visitors – were a common feature in these gardens, as were downhill water chains, musical water organs, 'water tables' on which the plates were floated during meals served *al fresco*, and statues of fantastic monsters, such as Giambologna's famous *Appennino* statue at the Villa Demidoff in Pratolino, above Florence. The very ethos of the Renaissance garden put it into a different category from the English garden, the creator of which, in Florence, had to battle not only

David Leavitt

Italian tradition but a climate and soil that could hardly have been more resistant to British imports. Georgina Grahame's 1902 memoir *In a Tuscan Garden* smacks of just the sort of jingoistic amateurism that sent McCarthy (and Wharton) over the edge. Such memoirs reek of colonialism – camphorated oil through which the ineradicable perfume of garlic, basil and tomatoes, set in a bowl of olive oil to sweat on a summer afternoon, persistently cuts.

Food was no less a problem for the Anglo-Florentines. Curiously enough, many of the English who moved to Florence at the turn of the last century distrusted and disdained Italian cuisine. Spaghetti – Forster's 'delicious slippery worms' – terrified them, because it defied years of training in how to eat politely. Although Ross's *Leaves from our Tuscan Kitchen* seems quaintly old-fashioned today, its very emphasis on fresh vegetables made it, in the meaty England of the late nineteenth century, an almost subversive text. As early as 1614, Giacomo Castelvetro, a Venetian exiled in England, had complained of a certain English coarseness when it came to preparing salads: 'You English are even worse [than "the Germans and other uncouth nations"],' he wrote;

> after washing the salad heaven knows how, you put the vinegar in the dish first, and enough of that for a footbath for Morgante, and serve it up, unstirred, with neither oil nor salt, which you are supposed to add at table. By this time some of the leaves are so saturated with vinegar that they cannot take the oil, while the rest are quite naked and fit only for chicken food.

By contrast, the Tuscans have always been great consumers of vegetables: eggplant, zucchini, legumes, spinach, borage, arugula and the famous Tuscan 'black cabbage' that is the basis of the Florentine soup known as *ribollita*. According to Castelvetro, the centrality of vegetables to the Italian diet owes in part to the fact that 'Italy, though beautiful, is not as plentifully endowed as France or this fertile island with meat, so we make it our business to devise other ways of feeding our excessive population.' The other reason he gives is that 'the heat, which persists for almost nine months of the year, has the effect of making meat seem quite repellent, especially beef, which in such a temperature one can hardly bear to look at, let alone eat'.

If today Florence is as famous for its immense steaks (*bistecche alla Fiorentina*) and slabs of roast pork (*arista*, a name derived, Norman Douglas tells us, from the Greek word for 'excellent') as it is for its vegetables, this is largely thanks to refrigeration. And yet vegetables continue to form the bulwark of the Florentine diet: chicory sautéed with hot peppers and garlic, white beans served at room temperature with fresh olive oil and pepper, cardoons (*cardi*) baked with cheese in a white sauce, not to mention the city's famous soups: *pappa al pomodoro*, a simple tomato soup thickened with bread, and *ribollita* – literally, 'reboiled', since the dish was traditionally prepared with the leftovers of a previous meal. A good *ribollita* is made with beans, carrots, onions, cabbage, hot red pepper, and leaves of Tuscan black cabbage, the whole thickened, as in *pappa al pomodoro*, with stale unsalted bread. Indeed, so mythic is this soup that at Cocco Lezzone, a Florentine *trattoria* said to be favored by Prince Charles, a note at the top of the menu warns patrons that 'the ringing of the cellular telephone may disturb the cooking of the *ribollita*'.

Of course, few of the original Anglo-Florentines ate *ribollita*, or anything else Italian: instead they depended on British shops to provide them with the staples necessary to approximate the dishes of home. At Lord Acton's, high tea was the customary social entertainment, with famously thin sandwiches. Even today, one can easily find Twining's tea, Walker's shortbread and Marmite in Florence, as shopkeepers cater to the English expatriate's nostalgia for home – a nostalgia that sometimes seems to border on xenophobia.

Their attitude toward dogs put them no less in conflict with the Italians, who even today tend to treat their dogs less as pets than as working animals. Indeed, the Anglo-Florentines may have introduced the idea of the *cane di compania* (the 'companion dog') into Italy. Vernon Lee's mother, Lady Paget, claimed to have settled in Florence because British quarantine laws did not permit her to take her beloved dachshund back to England. (She also

made her own shoes.) Ouida owned dozens of
dogs, which she was reputed to feed lobster,
petits-fours and cream from Capodimonte tea-
cups. An alternate version of her feud with
Janet Ross, offered by Moorehead, puts the
dogs at the center of the conflict; after one of
them bit her son, Ross had the dog punished,
provoking Ouida to retaliate by portraying
Lady Joan Challoner as a dog hater.

Florence remains, by Italian standards, a
remarkably dog-friendly city. When we lived
there, we used to have frequent encounters
with a madwoman who wore a white coat
over her nightgown and could be seen every
morning and every evening in the Piazza della
Signoria, walking four dogs on four leads:
small, nervous mongrels, one black, one
brindled, one the color of unwashed sheets,
and one pink, with a pink nose and an under-
bite. To any passing stranger who patted the
dogs' heads, or even smiled at them, this
woman would try to give one away, yet she
never seemed to find a taker. She would haul
them around for a while, then, quite suddenly,
let them go; leaping, they'd spread out over the
piazza, like the fingers of a splayed hand,

riding the crest of some race memory in which they frolicked with leopards whose spots formed tiny *fleurs-de-lis*, and wriggled between the legs of knights (one purple, one white), and urinated against trees the foliage of which rose up in staggered tiers, like the tiers of the metal platters that display coconut slices at Italian station bars, and which a drizzle of water moistens. Such furious little dogs, which have been breeding in Florence since its beginnings, can be found in Benozzo Gozzoli's frescoes in the Palazzo Medici-Riccardi, as well as in any number of Annunciations, Last Suppers, and battle scenes. It was the English, however, who took them to their hearts. Perhaps this madwoman is really Ouida's ghost.

Why Florence? Why not, instead, Paris, New York, Berlin, Naples, Vienna? The self-aggrandizing answer (and the one that casts the Anglo-Florentines in the most attractive light) is, again, that they came for art. A stance of rigorous scholarly asceticism seems to have been crucial to the image of themselves that they wanted to promulgate, something that

Forster captures perfectly when he has Reverend Eager describe to Lucy the residents of the villas they are passing as they ride into the hills. 'Lady Helen Laverstock is at present busy over Fra' Angelico,' he tells her. 'I mention her name because we are passing her villa on the left. No, you can only see it if you stand – no, do not stand; you will fall.' Another resident has written monographs for the series 'Medieval Byways'. Still another is 'working at Gemisthus Pletho'. True to type, Harold Acton translated *Gian Gastone* and Vernon Lee wrote something called *Euphorion; being Studies of the Antique and Medieval in the Renaissance*. These works served the function of giving the people back home the impression that their authors had a reason to be in Florence. They also distracted attention from the real reason so many of them had settled there: until the 1970s Florence was astonishingly, one might even say scandalously cheap. 'The villas are innumerable,' James wrote in 1877, most of them 'offered to rent (Many of them are for sale) at prices unnaturally low; you may have a tower and a garden, a chapel and an expanse of thirty windows, for five hundred dollars a year.' He goes on to wonder whether 'part of the brooding expression of these great houses' resulted from their 'having outlived their original use. Their extraordinary largeness and massiveness are a satire on their present fate. They weren't built with such a thickness of wall and depth of embrasure, such a solidity of staircase and superfluity of stone, simply to afford an economical winter residence to English and American families.'

A number of these were let to 'distressed gentlewomen'. Orioli recalls one of these, 'an old dear called Miss Lade', who lived alone with her dog and 'gave fancy-dress balls, ending in a supper of cold consommé which tasted like paint. Old as she was, she always dressed à la Carmen on such occasions – I suppose it was the only costume she still possessed, dating from the days of her youth. One day they found her asphyxiated in bed, with her dead dog beside her. She had tried to mend a leaking gas tube by herself, and had not succeeded.'

Although most of the colony's residents were English, there were also large numbers of Poles, French, Germans and Russians. This

David Leavitt

last group made a particularly vivid impression on the young Acton, who would later recall 'their church with the glittering onions off the Viale Milton . . .' Russian Grand Dukes and Duchesses visited frequently, as did significant Russian artists. In the 1870s, the Odessa-born pianist Vladimir de Pachmann was in Florence, studying with Vera Kologriv-off Rubio, who was married to the Florentine painter Luigi Rubio. In 1890 Tchaikovsky composed his opera *The Queen of Spades* in a hotel room overlooking the Arno. The writer Mikhail Kuzmin not only spent time in Florence, but set part of his 1906 novel *Wings* there. At one point he sends his hero, Vanya, on a tour led by a Tuscan Monsignor, who reveals to him the city's many social and economic strata:

Vanya met ruined *marchesi* and counts who lived in dilapidated palaces and quarreled with their servants over cards; he met engineers and doctors, merchants who lived the frugal, sequestered lives that their fathers had before them; he met budding composers who yearned for Puccini's fame, aping him with their neckties and fat, beardless faces; he met the Persian consul, fat, solemn and benign, who lived near San Miniato with his six nieces; he met apothecaries; he met young men who were vaguely described as errand boys, English ladies who had gone over to Catholicism and, finally, Mme. Monier, an aesthetic and artistic lady who lived in Fiesole with a whole company of guests in a villa decorated with charming allegories of spring and commanding a view of Florence and the Valley of the Arno. Invariably cheerful and eternally a-twitter, she was tiny, ginger-haired and quite hideous.

Kuzmin's account, with its catalogue of 'types', its reliance on semicolons, its faint whiff of a homosexual demimonde, is fairly typical of the period, yet it also suggests Florence's catholicity and richness of character. Although social barriers exist, for foreigners, they seem to melt on contact, so that Vanya can move from the houses of the aristocracy to those of the middle classes to those of artists and 'errand boys' with an ease that would be unthinkable at home. (The Monsignor's immunity to class distinction owes to his office;

no ordinary Italian could have made such a
pilgrimage.)

As for the English ladies 'who had gone over
to Catholicism', they may be the loudest presence of all. Even before the onslaught, Florentine society, with its entrenched aristocracy
and class-consciousness, was distinctly English
in tone, especially when compared to Rome or
Milan. As Acton writes, many of the old
Florentine families had 'Anglo-Saxon ramifications', which may have attracted the English.
'They took root among the vineyards and
became a part of the landscape,' he continues.
'Their eccentricities flourished in the clear
Tuscan light.' In *A Tuscan Childhood*, Kinta
Beevor, who grew up in Florence, wrote that
the city offered an 'escape from the hidebound
formality and false deference of home'; yet it
also replicated the atmosphere of home, in that
the region's much-vaunted relaxed attitude
came draped in the vestments of a social order
as hidebound as any to be found in England.
Thus in Florence, wealthy merchants were
obliged to address titled, though penniless,
aristocrats using the formal 'Loro'. The intri-
cate etiquette of correspondence amused

Forster, who in *Where Angels Fear to Tread* describes a letter sent by a young Tuscan to some English people:

Gino wrote in his own language, but the solicitors had sent a laborious English translation, where 'Pregiatissima Signorna' was rendered as 'Most Praiseworthy Madam', and every delicate compliment and superlative – superlatives are delicate in Italian – would have felled an ox.

More sensitive, perhaps, to the nuances of a world in which he spent only a few weeks than many of those who lived in it their whole lives, Forster appreciated the 'delicacy' of Tuscan society, which smiled on the very fluidities against which England was at that moment constructing dams. The smile was as subtle, as ambiguous, as the *Mona Lisa*'s, but it was a smile nonetheless. In Florence you could chat with a fellow expatriate at Doney's or La Giocosa, attend a formal ball at the *palazzo* of a Frescobaldi, and then at midnight stroll over to the Loggia dei Lanzi, where boys always loitered, happy to barter sex for money or cigarettes. What was absent was threat: the blackmailer's as much as the officer's. Firbank captured the town's split personality perfectly in a description, from *Sorrow in Sunlight* (1924), of the imaginary Caribbean capital Cuna-Cuna:

Now, beyond the Alemeda, in the modist faubourg of Faranaka, there lived a lady of both influence and wealth – the widow of the Inventor of Sunflower Piquant. The *veto* of Madame Ruis, arbitress absolute of Cunan society, and owner, moreover, of a considerable portion of the town, had caused the suicide indeed of more than one social climber. Unhappy, nostalgic, disdainful, selfish, ever about to abandon Cuna-Cuna to return to it no more, yet never budging, adoring her fairy villa far too well, Madame Ruiz [*sic*], while craving for the International-world, consoled herself by watching from afar European society going speedily to the dogs. Art-loving, and considerably musical (many a dizzy venture at the Opera-house had owed its audition to her), she had, despite the self-centredness of her nature, done not a little to render more brilliant the charming city it amused her with such vehemence to abuse.

Cuna-Cuna is also a city in which 'the number of ineligible young men or confirmed bachelors' provides 'a constant source of irritation' to mothers seeking husbands for their daughters.

CHAPTER THREE

Florence's reputation as a sodomitical hotbed goes way back. As early as the first years of the eighteenth century, (Henry James's cousin) H. Montgomery Hyde notes, an anonymous work titled *Plain Reasons for the Growth of Sodomy in England* was blaming 'women for the increase in homosexuality, besides foppish clothes, continental manners, tea-drinking and Italian opera'; the work also observed 'that sodomy is considered a trivial matter in Italy, since no sooner does a stranger set foot in Rome than the procurers rush to ask if he wants a woman or a young man'. A 1749 pamphlet titled *Satan's Harvest Home: or the Present State of Whorecraft, Adultery, Forni-*

cation, Procuring, Pimping and Sodomy . . . And Other Satanic Works, daily propagated in this good Protestant Kingdom stated the case more baldly, calling Italy the 'mother and nurse of sodomy'.

No doubt such diatribes had the opposite effect of what their authors intended; by vilifying Italy, they actually added to the country's appeal as a place of settlement for homosexual Englishmen obliged to flee their homeland. Among others, George Nassau Clavering-Cowper, third Earl Cowper – a Prince of the Holy Roman Empire and noted art collector, whom *The World* newspaper accused posthumously of having addicted himself 'to the practice and use of the most criminal and unmanly vices and debaucheries' – spent most of his life in Florence, where he died in 1789. In 1797 the Revd John Fenwick, Vicar of Byall, flew to France and then to Naples after a warrant was issued for his arrest on charges of assaulting a man named Harper, who had had to jump out of a library window in order to escape his attentions. In 1809, George Ferrers, Earl of Leicester, having been disinherited by his father after the exposure of an affair with a waiter called Neri (a Florentine name), settled in the Villa Rostan at Pegli, near Genoa. In 1841 William John Bankes, a parliamentarian, who had some years before been accused, Hyde writes, of 'committing an act of indecency with a soldier in a public lavatory outside Westminster Abbey', fled to Venice after he was brought to court a second time, for 'indecently exposing himself in a London park'.

Even before the adoption of the Code Napoléon – which, in contrast to English law, made a point of *not* criminalizing sodomy – Florence displayed an exceptionally permissive attitude toward homosexuality. Sodomy, if not homosexuality in the modern sense, had been a prominent feature of life in the city since at least the 1300s, when erotic relationships between men and boys were so prevalent that a special tribunal, the so-called 'Office of the Night', had had to be established to deal with the matter. In *Forbidden Friendships: Sodomy and Male Culture in Renaissance Florence*, the historian Michael Rocke describes a society in which sex between men and boys was tolerated so long as the passive partner was under eighteen. On the other hand, older men who took the passive role were looked upon as monstrous, and were often executed or maimed in public, their ears or noses cut off. The Ponte Vecchio, then the exclusive domain of butchers (it is now the exclusive domain of gold sellers), was something of a carnal war zone, a corridor down which no boy dared venture lest he should 'have his cap stolen'. By the early sixteenth century, a German dictionary was defining 'Florenzer' as 'buggerer' and the verb 'Florenzen' as 'to bugger'.

The city's twin status as a capital of great art and a haven of permissive sexual attitudes made it a particularly appealing destination for homosexual artists and scholars. Among the earliest of these to travel there was Winckelmann, the subject of a long chapter in *Studies on the History of The Renaissance*. 'In German imaginations,' Pater observed here, 'even now traces are to be found of that love of the sun, that weariness of the North (*cette fatigue du nord*), which carried the northern peoples away into those countries of the South.' (Many years later the young Sybille Bedford, crossing over the Brenner Pass, would likewise respond to 'the first sight on a September morning of a southern sky and light . . . with the alert joy of a creature born and emerging from the north'.) And what were these Germans – Winckelmann prominent among them – looking for? Art and love, 'the exercise of sight and touch', passionate friendships from which the erotic, bravely, was not excluded. 'There had been known before him,' Madame de Staël wrote of Winckelmann, 'learned men who might be consulted like books; but no one had, if I may say so, made himself a pagan for the purpose of penetrating antiquity.' Pater adds, 'That his affinity with Hellenism was not merely intellectual, that the subtler threads of temperament were inwoven in it, is proved by his romantic, fervent friendships with young men. He has known, he says, many young men more beautiful than Guido's archangel.'

Alas, the last of these friendships proved fatal; in 1768 Winckelmann decided to go back to Germany, traveled as far as Regensberg, then – homesick for Italy – cut his visit short and turned south again. Waiting in Trieste to sail, he fell in with a handsome café waiter, who murdered and robbed him in his hotel room. The waiter was Florentine, and his name, ironically, was Arcangeli.

The first edition of *The Renaissance* appeared in 1873, when Ouida was enjoying her greatest successes and trying, somewhat ineptly, to shock people at the Langham Hotel. This was a fraught moment in English social history, marked on the one hand by an increasing sexual boldness on the part of citizens, and on the other by a government-led effort to enforce sodomy laws as a defense against perceived Continental decadence. Among the earliest victims of the tension that resulted was Lord Henry Somerset, second son of the Duke of Beaufort (the Duke invented the game of Badminton, which was named after his estate) and the first of the so-called Uranian poets. A former MP for Monmouthshire and Comptroller of Her Majesty's Household, Lord Henry escaped England for Florence in the late 1870s after his wife, Isabel, caught him *in flagrante delicto* with a teenage boy named Harry Smith. Because she had gone public with the reasons for their separation, and thus flouted the Victorian code of 'reticence for women', Lady Isabel soon found herself *persona non grata* in English society. At home she became a pariah, while abroad, Lord Henry enjoyed (if that is the right word) an exile's odd notoriety; he is probably the 'suave Lord X' to whom Acton refers as having 'had to flee from the London police because he was a "Greek born out of due time" . . .' Then about ten years later Lord Henry's youngest brother, Arthur, was also obliged to flee for the Continent after being implicated in the famous 'Cleveland Street Scandal', which erupted in July 1889 when police stumbled upon a male brothel near Piccadilly staffed by telegraph boys, and catering to a generally aristocratic clientele. (Queen Victoria's grandson Prince Albert Victor, or 'Prince Eddy', the heir presumptive, was also reputed to have been a client at the brothel; certainly he was a frequent guest at the Hundred Guineas Club, a homosexual gathering place where he was known as 'Victoria'.)

The atmosphere in England had become especially oppressive since the 1885 passage of the Labouchère Amendment – named for

Henry Labouchère, the parliamentarian who wrote it, and who would soon become a member of the Anglo-Florentine colony in his own right, settling upon retirement at the Villa Cristina. (That he and Lord Henry should have ended up living cheek by jowl is further evidence of Florence's oddity, its status as a place outside the ordinary rules.) In essence, this amendment criminalized acts of 'gross indecency' between adult men in public or private, making them punishable by up to two years' imprisonment, with or without hard labor. (The maximum penalty was life imprisonment if minors were procured.) Previously, only anal intercourse – 'buggery' in England and 'sodomy' in Scotland – had been a crime.

Surprisingly, Labouchère was neither a religious zealot nor a conservative; on the contrary, he was a famous radical, the editor of a muckraking journal called *Truth* that was constantly being sued for libel. His amendment arrived in Parliament attached to a bill intended to curb the rise of syphilis among prostitutes, and was seen as contributory to an effort to contain this crisis. Previously, 'fallen women' themselves had been blamed for the ills associated with prostitution. Now lawmakers, at the urging of so-called 'social purity' feminists, were pushing the idea that the men at whose hands these women had 'fallen', rather than the women themselves, ought to be held accountable. According to this thinking, homosexual sex was simply the most extreme form that masculine depravity could take; men who engaged in acts of 'gross indecency' with each other, rather than categorisable 'inverts', were monsters of carnality, as likely to go hunting girl virgins to corrupt as to soil together the beds of decent hotels. Desire itself, in other words, was the crime that had to be punished.

The problem, of course, was that outside the imagination of Victorian physiologists, such polysexual demons as those at whom the law was aimed did not, by and large, exist. 'Inverts', on the other hand, were legion, and in the end it was they who suffered the most from the Labouchère amendment, in great part thanks to the words 'in public or private', which were seen as giving the green light to blackmailers, and soon led to its being dubbed the 'blackmailer's charter'. Oscar Wilde's 1895 arrest under the amendment's provisions sent homosexuals into a panic, and provoked the rather fantastic exodus that Frank Harris describes in his inventive biography of Wilde:

Every train to Dover was crowded; every steamer to Calais thronged with members of the aristocratic and leisured classes, who seemed to prefer Paris, or even Nice out of the season, to a city like London, where the police might act with such unexpected vigour . . . It came as a shock to their preconceived ideas that the police in London knew a great many things which they were not supposed to concern themselves with, and this unwelcome glare of light drove the vicious forth in wild haste.

Florence was where most of them landed, since it offered, as Barbara Strachey primly put it in her memoir *Remarkable Relations*, 'an ideal place for the unconventional Anglo-Saxon at this time. Lord Henry Somerset . . . had taken refuge there . . . and the large expatriate community abounded in "Sapphists", eccentrics and those whose marital arrangements were irregular.'

She was neither generalizing nor indulging in overstatement. The lesbians in residence included, most notably, Radclyffe Hall, author of the banned novel *The Well of Loneliness*, who lived in Florence with her lover, Una, Lady Troubridge. Then there was the travel writer Maud Cruttwell, who dressed in men's clothes and told Mary Berenson 'how pleased she was to ride behind my donkey when she thought it was a female ass, and how disgusted she was when she found out it was a "maschio"'. The Florence-born Violet Paget, known as Vernon Lee, kept her hair cropped short and, like Maud Cruttwell, wore a man's necktie. James described her as 'exceedingly ugly, disputatious, contradictious and perverse . . . a really superior talker with a *mind* – almost the only one in Florence'. Likewise the German sculptor Adolf von Hildebrand recalled in a letter a dull evening enlivened by her intellectual vigor:

During the dinner there was desultory chat; then we sat out till half past eleven near the little gate and I had a long discussion with Vernon Lee on the nature of truth. She was very aggressive and

brilliantly intelligent, and after two hours succeeded in proving triumphantly the very state-
ment she had undertaken to combat . . .

John Singer Sargent painted her portrait; her
writing impressed Pater, and she enjoyed a
long if rivalrous friendship with Berenson,
who held court, with his wife Mary, at I Tatti.
Visitors streamed in and out of the villa,
among the oddest of them the poet Michael
Field, not one man but two women, an aunt
and niece named Katharine Bradley and Edith
Cooper, who lived together from the time that
Edith was a small child until her death in 1913.
(Katharine died a year later.) Of 'the Mikes', as
they were not so affectionately known, Mary
Berenson wrote:

They think they are a Great Poet, unappreciated
at present but certain to be famous and adored in
the next generation – and they think their souls
are united and that it is good for them to be
together. As a matter of fact the utter mistake of
both these theories is 'obvious to the meanest
intelligence' . . .

(A stanza from their interminable 'Variations on Sappho' proves the point:

> Maids, not to you my mind doth change;
> Men I defy, allure, estrange,
> Prostrate, make bond or free:
> Soft as the stream beneath the plane
> To you I sing my love's refrain;
> Between us is no thought of pain,
>   Peril, satiety.)

Berenson's own marriage to Mary, as it happened, was among the more 'irregular' in Florence, encompassing a relatively open *ménage à trois* of which the third member was his female secretary, Nicky Mariano. Heterosexual members of the colony, it seemed, had reasons no less pressing for living in Italy. Thus the Hon. Mrs George Keppel, former mistress to King Edward VII and mother of yet another lesbian, the novelist Violet Trefusis, settled with her patient husband at the Villa dell'Ombrellino in Bellosguardo. (What choice did she have besides Florence?) Lord Arthur Acton was a zealous amateur photographer in the tradition of Baron von Gloeden, except that his nude subjects were young girls instead of, as in von Gloeden's case, (mostly) young boys; as the novelist Francis King recalled in *Yesterday came Suddenly*, he 'had been involved in a scandal before the First World War, when the police were tipped off by a mother dissatisfied with her pay-off that, along with a local politician, he was photographing pubescent girls in a studio rented for that purpose'. He also fathered numerous illegitimate children by Florentine women, one of whom would later sue for half his estate. Yet for all his indiscretions, Arthur showed little tolerance toward his son, who even in his late forties was allowed neither use of the family car (he took the bus instead) or his own key to the villa; instead, James Lord writes in 'The Cost of the Villa', whenever Harold returned late at night, he would have to clamber up the wall and enter by a window.

Although today he is better remembered for his memoirs and his history of the Bourbons of Naples, Acton also wrote three novels – *Humdrum, Peonies and Ponies*, and *New Lamps for Old* – as well as numerous forgotten short stories, including one called 'The Soul's Gymnasium'. Here a mad old man in orange robes tries to persuade young male visitors to his Florentine garden to 'doff their worldly garments' and dive into a 'pool of purification'. The second of these young men, an American named Al Randy, has earlier 'doffed' his garments to pose naked alongside a copy of the *David*, to whose physique his own compares favorably.

Acton's homosexuality was an open secret in Florence – which did not stop him from threatening a lawsuit when he heard that he was to be 'outed' in a biography of Nancy Mitford. (His putative motive was to protect the delicate sensibilities of Prince Charles and Princess Diana, who had recently stayed at La Pietra.) In two long volumes of memoirs, he never once acknowledged his own homosexuality, though he spoke often of homosexuality in the abstract – in the first volume, for instance, writing, 'One was continually hearing that certain men in Florence were queer, not that it made much difference to their popularity: on the contrary! The queerer, the dearer.' Significantly, the subject of this observation, rather than himself or one of his lovers, is a stranger glimpsed at a distance, and identified by a *female* companion as queer. 'But wherein did this queerness reside?' Acton asks disingenuously.

> I must find out. In trying to solve this problem I stared at the young man until he flushed with embarrassment. 'But I can't see anything queer about him,' I exclaimed, and was told to mind my own business, which led to further cogitation. Thinking him over, I came to the conclusion that he was prettier than a man was supposed to be; and that might have something to do with it. But how could he help having curly hair and a pink and white complexion? If he shaved his head and wore a beard he might look more manly, of course, but wouldn't that be rather affected?

Were it not for the fact that he was in no way pretty, Acton might have been talking about himself here; far from a minor 'problem to be solved', queerness was for him a dilemma requiring the use of an ever-more complex algebra of evasion – thus the displacement of homosexuality, in the memoirs, on to a remote (and 'safe') third party, or the observa-

tion, when assessing the failed marriages of
some of his friends, 'I could congratulate my-
self on being a bachelor.' ('As if the option had
been exercised after dispassionate contempla-
tion!' James Lord notes wryly.) During the
Second World War, Acton had been refused
a post in Peking, where he had lived in his
youth, due to a report claiming that his beha-
vior there had been less than that befitting an
officer and a gentleman. Resentment of this
'slander' still burned in 1968, and in the introduction to *More Memoirs of an Aesthete*,
Acton characterizes the author of the denunci-
ation as 'some epicene dunderhead from the
Foreign Office. His rage against my indepen-
dent way of life was that of the perennial snake
in the grass, the envious Philistine.' In analyz-
ing this passage, Lord points out that in general usage the definition of 'epicene' is
effeminate. 'How can Harold have been so
rash as to attribute to his accuser a character-
istic which must have been central to the
accusation against himself?' Lord asks. 'Did
he actually fancy that no one knew?'

It's hard to imagine, just as it's hard to
imagine that Pino Orioli really believed he

was fooling anyone when he described in *Adventures of a Bookseller* a dispute that arose between him and his partner Davis after they fell in love with the same 'creature' – a 'creature' whose gender, in the course of a long passage, is never specified. (Italian, with its evasive articles, is even more pliant than English in this game of gender obfuscation.) Yet Orioli shows no similar reticence when lamenting the superfluity of 'Geoffreys' passing through Florence 'singly or in couples', since the observation does not implicate him:

> Not all of them are called Geoffrey, but most of them bear that name which, somehow or other, suits them perfectly. The name conjures up for me the vision of a young fellow, generally from an English University, generally arriving in his own or a friend's car, generally effeminate; always well dressed, always rich, and always close with his money. . . . Decorative boys but quite empty-headed, and rather a nuisance into the bargain.

(Along the same lines, a character in Jocelyn Brooke's 'Gerald Brockhurst' makes the observation that in novels as well as life, 'Geralds' are almost inevitably athletic and straight: 'There's one in E. M. Forster, and another in Lawrence – you know, the man in *Women in Love* – and I once read a novel by Gilbert Frankau, when I was at school, called *Gerald Cranston's Lady*; the hero was just the same type, terrifically hearty and military, with a mustache.')

For Orioli as much as for Acton, it was one thing to observe the faintly embarrassing ways of foreigners, and another to talk about oneself. Thus Orioli can recall a group of Germans who 'used to meet every afternoon at a certain table – it happened to be square and not round – in the Café Gambrinus, which was the most fashionable at the time . . . If you passed near them, you could hear one or the other of them saying charming things about Donatello or Dante or Michelangelo or Bruno or Benvenuto. If you took a table near enough to overhear what they were saying, you soon realized that they were not comparing the merits of those famous Italians of bygone days, but those of the best-looking modern youngsters about town who bore the same names.'

Of course, it is about as easy to believe that Orioli merely 'took a table near enough to overhear' this conversation as that Proust, in *Time Regained*, chose by chance a gay brothel when he decided to check into a hotel to take a rest. Far more probable is that Orioli was sitting with the Germans, taking part in their conversation, as entranced by the boys with the artists' names as they were.

Among the most entrenched relics of the homosexual community in Florence during the first part of the twentieth century was Lord Henry Somerset, who – following his flight from England – settled at 1 Via Guido Monaco, not far from the station of Santa Maria Novella. In prelapsarian days, Lord Somerset had not done much of anything; now he became slightly famous as a songwriter ('All Through the Night', 'The First Spring Day', 'Where'er You Go', etc.). He was also the author of a slim volume of verse, *Songs of Adieu* (1889), inspired by his great love Harry Smith, who would die in New Zealand in 1902. Here is one of these poems, entitled 'The Exile':

Florence, A Delicate Case

O PRAY for me!
That weeping stand on a distant shore,
My young days darkened for evermore –
    O pray for me!
Pray for the homeless, outcast one,
Pray for the life crushed out and done
Ere yet its youth had scarce begun –
    O pray for me!

    O think of me!
I loved you well in the days gone by,
Together, you said, we'd live and die –
    O think of me!
Think then of those imperial years,
Think, think of all my bitter tears,
My racking doubts, my dismal tears –
    O think of me!
Yea, dear one, morning, noon, and night,
I think, and weep, and pray for thee,
And through my tears my one delight
Is born of thy dear memory.
My life with thine is past and o'er,
We can but weep for evermore.

Oscar Wilde, reviewing the *Songs of Adieu* in
the *Pall Mall Gazette* of 30 March 1889,

concluded, 'He has nothing to say and says it'; a quip that did not keep Somerset from entertaining Wilde when he came to Florence to visit Lord Alfred Douglas in 1894. 'Podge', as Somerset was known, was as tragicomic an eccentric as the hero of 'The Soul's Gymnasium'. Osbert Sitwell, who made something of a career out of memorializing Anglo-Florentine dinosaurs, portrayed him as 'Milordo Inglese' in one of the poems that comprise 'On the Continent', the third section of his 1958 collection *Poems about People*, or *England Reclaimed*. Here Podge is 'Lord Richard Vermont', whom 'some nebulous but familiar scandal / Had lightly blown ... over the Channel, / Which he never crossed again.'

Thus at the age of twenty-seven
A promising career was over,
And the thirty or forty years that had elapsed
Had been spent in killing time – or so Lord
    Richard thought,
Though in reality, *killing time*
Is only the name for another of the
    multifarious ways
By which time kills us.

Florence, A Delicate Case

Lord Richard's house – 'a miniature castle of plaster / Coloured and divided by lines to represent red brick' – is protected by a door that 'was bolted in ten places, / And only un-barred after a footman / Had scanned your face and the horizon / Through a slot in the door':

Once you were allowed to enter, you were
    lost in a dark, gleaming forest
Of golden pillars: a herald's paradise;
There were many little rooms, studded with
    coats-of-arms:
But though it was an ingenious, confusing
    forest, with reflections everywhere in mirrors,
It was yet a work of artifice, not of art;
    There was one room, copper-sheeted,
    Which blushed to rose when the lights
      turned on,
And another in which the walls
    Were sheets of transparent glass –
    I thought it might be to remind him not
      to throw stones,
        But he explained,
    'I wanted to see what it would be like,
      dear boy,
    To live in a room with no walls.'

Sitwell's sketch – with the exception of a small cache of letters, the most substantial portrait of Lord Somerset to survive – concludes with Lord Richard as an old man receiving guests in a bathroom at the top of his castle, dispensing coffee instead of tea ' "Because tea," he would say, as he poured out the coffee, / "Is responsible for all the dreadful scandal / Talked in English drawing-rooms." ' The poem's last lines emphasize the somewhat wistful unreality of these final days, describing the little that remains of Lord Richard's 'solitary splendor' as 'wings of dust / Enclosing an untenanted miniature castle / With stained walls / In a wisteria-strangled suburb.'

Lord Richard's attempt, in Florence, to create 'a room with no walls' finally meets with failure because he has confused artifice with art, fancy with invention. This was a common mistake among the Anglo-Florentines, and one of the chief reasons that so many of them ended up mired in mediocrity. As Edward Prime-Stevenson observed in his underground study *The Intersexes*, the sexual liberty enjoyed by homosexual émigrés in Italy 'seems remarkably often to have had the effect of destroying their intellectual or artistic activity and ambition. They become professional drifters and "dawdlers", degenerate in will, in purpose, and even inter-sexual virility. They do nothing, accomplish nothing, while constantly talking about doing and accomplishing; and anon having lapsed gently to idleness complete, the capital of talent seems to evaporate away. Their liberty really gained, its relief undoes them.'

Another of Sitwell's portraits, 'Mr Algernon Petre', is about Reggie Temple, a member of the colony often confused with the novelist Reggie Turner, as Algy Petre, in the poem, is often confused with the novelist Algy Braithwaite. 'Boxes', the third section of the poem, addresses Temple/Petre's vocation as the maker of small decorative *objets*:

Completely
  Undeterred
By the various gigantic figures
That threw shadows across his path here –
  So that, every morning, before beginning
    work,
      He had, as it were, to sweep out of his
        enormous Studio

David Leavitt

> The spectres of Leonardo and
>   Michelangelo –
> Algy Petre settled down for over fifty years,
> Through summer and short winter,
> To paint the identical, highly polished
>   portrait of Queen Marie Antoinette
>   On the lids
>   Of diminutive circular boxes,
>   Subsequently lacquered.

Ignoring Leonardo, Algy Petre looks back to the age of Verrocchio, 'the perfection', in Pater's words (which echo here), 'of the older Florentine style of miniature-painting, with patient putting on of each leaf upon the trees and each flower in the grass . . .' In Sitwell's summing up, Temple/Petre is portrayed as having spent his life 'Contentedly working by a method / That, before he rediscovered it, / Had fortunately been forgotten':

> Painting the portrait of someone he had never
>   seen,
>   Until it was time for him, too, to fold up
>   Into a box he had not painted,
>   Under a cypress tree.

His boxes – precious and pointless – might be said to emblemize the colony itself, just as Algy Petre might be said to embody its spirit. For him, the ghosts of greatness are suspiciously easy to dispel. He is a dilettante, yet unlike Lord Richard Vermont, who seeks to create a room without walls, he boxes himself in: opposed methods that lead to the same fate.

Sitwell also included in his collection a *poeme-à-clef* about Reginald Turner, an unsuccessful novelist but much-loved man, and one of Oscar Wilde's intimates. (He had been at Wilde's bedside when the poet died.) Here Turner is portrayed as Braithwaite, 'a friend of Wilde and Whistler' who 'Had lived abroad for many years, / Making a small income go a little way.' It is not a kind poem:

When he laughed – which was often –
His ugly sallow face
    Would collapse into a thousand wrinkles,
And his eyes, those dejected cornflowers,
    Would wink, blink and water.

Although he was himself the author of almost as many books as Ouida – among them *Castles*

David Leavitt

in Kensington, Count Florio and Phyllis K.
and *Samson Unshorn* – Turner is perhaps best
remembered for a quip: when W. Somerset
Maugham complained to him that he could
find no first editions of his novels, he replied,
'Really? I can't find any second editions of
mine.' (Maugham, not incidentally, was a
frequent visitor to Florence in those days,
usually in the company of his secretary, Gerald
Haxton.) Like Acton, Turner suffered a fate
typical to many of the Anglo-Florentines, that
of being better remembered for the people he
had known than for anything he himself had
done. In this regard his connection with Wilde
was a source of vexation to him. Acton recalls
a French novelist, André Germain, embarrassing Turner 'by seizing his hand and clinging to
it while he piped in a shrill octave: "*Ai-je bien
l'honneur de parler avec le grand ami d'Oscar
Wilde? Monsieur, permettez-moi de vous em-
brasser.*" ' On another occasion 'Ronald Firbank, whose mere voice made Reggie wince,
rushed upon him from a flower-shop and
covered him from head to foot with lilies.'

Turner was a close friend of Norman Douglas, whom Sitwell called 'Donald McDougall'

in yet another poem. In those years, Douglas spent much of his time on Capri, which was then to Florence what Fire Island is now to New York. He wrote a novel set in Capri's expatriate community – *South Wind* – as did Compton McKenzie, the founder of *The Gramophone*. (His was called *Vestal Fire*.) Under a pseudonym – 'Pilaf Bey' – Douglas also published a collection of aphrodisiac recipes, *Venus in the Kitchen*, for which Graham Greene provided the introduction.

Much innuendo surrounded Douglas's murky sexual life. In *The Ant Colony*, Francis King's gossipy novel about Florence, an Italian named Franco recalls Douglas gathering around him 'some pubescent schoolboys, Franco among them', while holding aloft 'a note of pitifully small denomination to be awarded to the boy who, in an increasingly frenzied contest, succeeded in coming first'. Acton described to James Lord the walking tours that he would sometimes take through Chianti with Scott Moncrieff and Douglas, 'who could not be kept from fondling little boys in every village they passed through'. This habit finally caught up with the elderly writer during the Fascist era, when he was run out of Florence as a result of his involvement with a twelve-year-old boy. Although Acton wrote about the episode in his memoirs, in a skewed attempt to protect his friend's reputation (or perhaps his own) he changed the boy to a girl, thus giving Compton McKenzie the opportunity to quip, 'They all turn to little girls in the end.'

Ronald Firbank's personal eccentricities have subsumed, for many readers, the genuine interest of his work. To the painter Duncan Grant, he was 'an elegant grasshopper in white kid gloves and boots'; to Carl Van Vechten, his friend and champion, an 'Aubrey Beardsley in a Rolls-Royce', a 'Jean Cocteau at the Savoy'. Even Firbank took part in the cult of his own persona, complaining in a letter to Van Vechten that reviews made him feel 'quite like a bottle of prohibition whiskey, & not at all like the *Veuve Cliquot* (1886), special cuvée' that he knew himself to be.

In *Noble Essences*, Osbert Sitwell recalls that 'during the April and May when [Firbank] was living in a villa that had formerly belonged to the Swiss painter Böcklin, situated outside Florence', Sitwell and his brother Sachaverell would often encounter him in the Via Tornabuoni, 'staggering under a load of flowers he had bought, and craning round in a wild and helpless way for a cab to carry him home . . .' Flowers figure prominently as well in Acton's description of the meeting between Firbank and Reggie Turner, who disliked him intensely. 'Though Firbank led an isolated life,' Acton continues,

maintaining no more than a jerky acquaintance with a few choice relics of the 'nineties who did not know what to make of him, nobody has conveyed the aroma of Florentine gossip better than he. He endeared himself to the waiters at Betti's by his handsome tips. Having carefully ordered fruit that was out of season, he would sit and contemplate it like an El Greco Saint in ecstasy. Muscat grapes in mid-winter he would dangle against the light, eyeing the clusters caressingly as he sipped glass after glass of wine. At the food he merely picked and jabbed as if it repelled him.

In short, Firbank was the perfect avatar of *fin de siècle* decadence, just as the style that he perfected – distinguished by a self-reflexive archness that echoes the barbed intercourse of Florence – represents the most extreme manifestation of the movement that Wilde (and to a lesser extent Beardsley) had initiated several decades earlier. Nor is the association between Firbank and Wilde merely literary. During his youth, Firbank managed to maintain longstanding friendships both with Lord Alfred Douglas and with Wilde's son Vyvyan Holland, whose twenty-first birthday party he attended, as did Henry James. (Later, according to his biographer, Miriam Benkowitz, 'Firbank snubbed [Holland] for his pleasure at a series of lawsuits which Douglas lost.') By employing the Wildean voice, which was also the voice of café chat at Doney's, Firbank was able to subvert not only Anglo-Florentine self-promotion, but English attitudes generally.

Of all his novels, the one that shows the strongest Florentine influence is *The Flower Beneath the Foot*, most of which he wrote while renting the Villa I Lecci at 15 Via Benedeto di Maiano in Fiesole. 'How different my book would have been had I gone to Vienna,' he wrote to his mother, 'for of course one's surroundings tell. Probably it would have been more brilliant & flippant, but not so good as the steady work I hope to do here.' He saw his own style in the novel as being 'vulgar, cynical & "horrid"', but of course beautiful here & there for those that can see'. Such writing as his own, he felt, must bring 'discomfort to fools, since it is aggressive, witty & unrelenting'.

It will come as no surprise that *The Flower Beneath the Foot* is a *roman-à-clef*. To the *habitués* of the fictitious Pisuerga, where the novel takes place, Firbank prepared a kind of cheat sheet, which he sent to his mother:

'Princess Elsie' = Princess Mary. 'Mrs Chilleywater' = Mrs Harold Nicolson. 'Eddy' = Evan Morgan – & of course 'King Geo' & 'Queen Glory' are the king & queen. The English ambassadress is founded on Mrs Roscoe & Lady Nicolson . . . The lady journalist must be 'Eve' of the *Tatler* or any other of the prattling busybodies that write for the magazine.

Princess Mary was visiting Fiesole on her honeymoon at the time that Firbank was writing *The Flower Beneath the Foot*. Other connections ink themselves in as the novel progresses. Madame Wetme, the owner of a Doney's-like bar, longs above all else to get into society; her 'religion, her cruel God, was the *Chic*: the God Chic'. Even Madame Wetme's metaphors reflect Florentine geography: 'I admit we live in the valley,' she tells a Duchess. 'Although *I* have a great sense of the hills!'

In-joke nicknames abound. One conversation alone features 'Grim-lips and Ladybird, Hairy and Fluffy, Hardylegs and Bluewings, Spindleshanks and Our Lady of Furs'. At another moment the King of Pisuerga, upon being informed during a banquet that in the imaginary country of Dateland there is no such thing as china, replies, 'I could not be more astonished . . . if you told me there were fleas at the Ritz.' This chance remark, misunderstood by Lady Something, the British ambassadress, becomes the stuff of wild rumor, and eventually results in the owners of the Ritz suing her for libel.

Firbank saves his most biting parody for the aesthete 'Eddy' Monteith, son of Lord Intriguer, a character based on his former intimate, Evan Morgan. In 1920, the two had had a falling-out over Firbank's play *The Princess Zoubaroff*, which he wanted to dedicate to Morgan. At first Morgan accepted his friend's offer with gratitude; shortly before publication, however, he had a change of heart, and threatened to sue Firbank's publisher, Grant Richards, if the dedication was not removed. (One is reminded of James's horrified protests when Forest Reid dedicated *The Garden God* to him.) Writing *The Flower Beneath the Foot*, Firbank no doubt still nursed a grudge, for he ridicules Morgan's 'aesthetic' tendencies:

Lying amid the dissolving bath crystals while his manservant deftly bathed him, he fell into a sort of coma, sweet as a religious trance. Beneath the rhythmic sponge, perfumed with *Kiki*, he was St Sebastian, and as the water became cloudier, and the crystals evaporated amid the steam, he was Teresa . . . and he would have been, most likely, the Blessed Virgin herself but that the bath grew gradually cold.

Eddy is the author of a volume of *Juvenilia*, the contents of which includes such works as 'Lines to Doris: written under the influence of wine, sun and fever', 'Ode to Swinburne', 'Sad Tamarisks', 'Rejection', 'Doigts Obscènes', 'They Call Me Lily!!' and 'Land of Titian! Land of Verdi! O Italy!' Later, and in a footnote, no less, Eddy dies while taking part in an archaeological dig near Sodom: 'the shock received by meeting a jackal while composing a sonnet had been too much for him . . . Alas, for the *triste* obscurity of his end!'

Another interesting character in *The Flower Beneath the Foot* is Count Cabinet, a ' "fallen" minister of the Crown exiled to the island of St Helena'. Though the nature of the scandal is never specified, nor his name included in the 'who's who' of the novel that Firbank sent his mother, Count Cabinet's banishment calls to mind strongly the fate of Lord Henry Somerset. When the righteous Countess of Tolga takes a boat to 'intrude upon the flattered exile', she brings as a gift 'a pannier of well-grown, early pears, a small "heath" and the Erotic Poems, bound in half calf with tasteful tooling, of a Schoolboy poet, cherishable chiefly perhaps for the vignette frontispiece of the author'. Count Cabinet lives alone on his island except for his 'useful' secretary, Peter Passer, whom Firbank describes as 'more valet perhaps than secretary, and more errand-boy than either'. According to his account, the 'former chorister of the Blue Jesus' volunteered to follow 'the fallen statesman into exile at a moment when the Authorities of Pisuerga were making minute enquiries for sundry missing articles, from the *Trésor* of the Cathedral . . .' (Perhaps some eighteenth-century vestments, in which young Peter went around dressed as Cardinal Richelieu?)

Firbank's account of the pair occasions some of his loveliest prose. While fishing from an open window, Count Cabinet, to his surprise, catches 'a distinguished mauvish fish with vivid scarlet spots', the sight of which provokes him to ponder 'on the mysteries of the deep, and of the subtle variety that is in Nature . . . Among the more orthodox types that stocked the lake, such as carp, cod, tench, eels, sprats, shrimps, etc., this exceptional fish must have known its trials and persecutions . . . And the Count, with a stoic smile, recalled his own.' Like Wilde, the 'distinguished fish' is both stoic and beautiful in the face of adversity and dislocation.

Indeed, as Firbank describes it, the isle of the Count's exile is almost Edenic in its tranquil (and Mediterranean) beauty. Here, when not 'boating or reading or feeding his swans, to watch Peter's fancy-diving off the terrace end was perhaps the favorite pastime of the veteran *viveur*'.

To behold the lad trip along the riven break-water, as naked as a statue, shoot out his arms and spring, the *flying-head-leap* or the *Back-sadilla*, was a beautiful sight, looking up now and again – but more often now – from a volume of old Greek verse; while to hear him warbling in the water with his clear alto voice – of Kyries and Anthems he knew no end – would often stir the old man to the point of tears. Frequently the swans themselves would paddle up to listen, expressing by the charmed or rapturous motions of their necks (recalling to the exile the ecstasies of certain musical or 'artistic' dames at Concert-halls, or the Opera House, long ago) their mute appreciation, their touched delight . . .

Among the 'strangely gorgeous' swans on whom the Count dotes, one pecks at Peter, 'Jealous, doubtless of the lad's grace.' The boy, 'naked as a statue', is in his nudity the very paragon of the artificial. For the Count, as for Baron von Gloeden, Classicism justifies polite pornography, just as in *The Garden God*, the 1905 novel for which James refused a dedication, a boy called Graham poses his friend Harold in the attitudes of the faun, the *spinario*, the *Adorante*, and a youthful Dionysius with a face 'like that of Leonardo's Bacchus'. Once again, we are in Florence.

Toward the end of *The Flower Beneath the Foot*, Firbank lapses into a Proustian meditation on dusk that is not without its elements of Wildean paradox. 'In certain lands,' he observes, 'with what diplomacy falls the night, and how discreetly is the daylight gone.

These dimmer-and-dimmer, darker-and-lighter twilights of the North, so disconcerting in their playfulness, were unknown altogether in Pisuerga. There, Night pursued Day as though she meant it. No lingering or arctic sentiment! No concertina-ishness . . . Hard on the sun's heels

David Leavitt

pressed Night. And the wherefore of her haste;
Sun-attraction? Impatience to inherit? An answer to such riddles as these may doubtless be
found by turning to the scientist's theories on
Time and Relativity.

Instead of calling attention to the frozenness of
the North, or using its unyielding winters as a
metaphor for moral intolerance, Firbank here
emphasizes the 'playfulness' of Northern
dusks; in his hands, even the cold becomes
invested with 'arctic sentiment'. In the South,
on the other hand, sunset is as brusque, as
brutal, as an Italian farmwoman efficiently
slaughtering a chicken. Night pursues day
'as if she meant it' (just as Count Cabinet
has been pursued), issuing a lights-out order
on his island paradise, and reminding us that
banishment, even to the loveliest Gulag, is
never without its acrid flavor.

All great writers are finally transformers,
rather than scribes, of experience. Unlike Acton, who does little more than repeat the old
gossip, or Sitwell, who makes of it a salon
comedy, Firbank formulated from the Floren-

tine penchant for arch humor and social spite a unique literary strategy. An acute historian of the expatriate English in southern Europe (and elsewhere), he was also the most important advocate of a literary style the influence of which is far-reaching, revealing itself not only in the subtle satire of Muriel Spark and David Lodge (both of whom live in Tuscany), but in a whole tradition of homosexually themed fiction the practitioners of which, from Alfred Chester to Edmund White, owe a debt (sometimes acknowledged) to his legacy. In this regard, he justifies the more trivial of the Anglo-Florentine writers, most of whom have fallen into an obscurity as complete as that of his own weed-choked grave in Rome. Though future generations of readers will probably not recognize his name, they will feel, in the pages of the writers to whom he mattered, and the writers to whom they mattered, the subtle pull and pressure of his wit.

CHAPTER FOUR

No image in the history of Western art, with the possible exception of the *Mona Lisa*, has been reproduced as frequently as Michelangelo's *David*. In Florence especially, his *doppelgängers* proliferate – Luigi Arighetti's marble copy on Piazza della Signoria, Clemente Papi's bronze copy on Piazzale Michelangelo, not to mention the mass-produced replicas in plaster of Paris, plastic, brass, and even onyx (a black *David*) on sale in the city's gift shops, one of which is called 'David's Shop'. A copy of the statue stands guard at the city's gay sauna, as at many other gay saunas in Europe. Outside the Palazzo Vecchio, postcard vendors peddle every conceivable view of the David, as well as aprons printed with his torso, underwear printed with his crotch, postcards in which he and the fat Bacchus from the Boboli Gardens are juxtaposed under the heading 'Before and After', and perhaps most trashily, close-up shots of his genitals, some with cartoon sunglasses perched over the pubic hair and the words 'WOW! FLORENCE!' added near the top. Two years ago, for my birthday, my brother gave me a magnetized *David* paper doll whose varied wardrobe (speedos, dinner jacket, tank top and shorts) would have better suited an urban homosexual of the early nineteen-eighties than a Biblical hero or even an athletic Florentine boy at the end of the fifteenth century. Such vulgarizations, like Marcel Duchamp's famous mustaching of the *Mona Lisa*, suggest a discomfort with the sublimity of great works of art, a desire to diminish their intensity through defacement or ridicule. At the same time, they attest to the statue's carnal force, that physicality to which Pater gave voice when he wrote that Michelangelo 'loved the very quarries of Carrara, those strange grey peaks which even at mid-day convey into any scene from which they are visible something of the solemnity and stillness of evening, sometimes wandering among them month after month, till at last their pale ashen colours seem to have passed into his painting; and on the crown of the head of the *David* there still remains a morsel of uncut stone, as if by one touch to maintain his connexion with the place from which it was hewn'.

Now, examining the reproduction of the *David*'s face on a mousepad I purchased the other day at the Museum of the Opera del Duomo, I see the 'morsel' to which Pater refers. David's expression is at once fretful and uncertain, as if he is questioning the very act of slingshot heroism for which he will be memorialized. In the reproductions, Mark notes, this look that dances on the edge of contrition hardens into something more like churlishness, and the face becomes pinched and mean. The real *David*, by contrast, has an odd delicacy about him, even a fragility, of which his very massiveness is the paradoxical source. What might be called the *David*'s prehistory is illustrative in this regard. The five-meter stone slab from which he was carved had originally been quarried in 1464 for the

Opera del Duomo, but was never used because the sculptor who had blocked it out, to quote a contemporary of Michelangelo's, was 'insufficiently acquainted with his art'. Some years later, the sculptor Andrea Sansovino tried to persuade the board of the Opera del Duomo to let him have a go at it; only Michelangelo, however, offered a proposal that did not require the addition of other pieces of stone, and for this reason, the marble was given to him. (Indeed, it is because of the exactitude with which Michelangelo made use of this slab that the morsel of uncut stone on the *David*'s head remains.)

'In the *David* Michelangelo first displayed that quality of *terribilità*, of spirit-quailing, awe-inspiring force, for which he afterwards became so famous,' John Addington Symonds wrote in his biography of the artist:

> The statue imposes, not merely by its size and majesty and might, but by something vehement in the conception. . . . Wishing perhaps to adhere strictly to the Biblical story, Michelangelo studied a lad whose frame was not developed. The *David*, to state the matter

frankly, is a colossal hobbledehoy. [Theophile
Gautier wrote that he looked like 'a market-
porter'.] His body, in breadth of the thorax,
depth of the abdomen, and general stoutness,
has not grown up to the scale of the enormous
hands and feet and heavy head. We feel that
he wants at least two years to become a fully
developed man, passing from adolescence to
the maturity of strength and beauty. This
close observance of the imperfections of the
model at a certain stage of physical growth is
very remarkable, and not altogether pleasing
in a statue more than nine feet high. Both
Donatello and Verrocchio had treated their
*David*s in the same realistic manner, but they
were working on a small scale and in bronze. I
insist upon this point, because students of
Michelangelo have been apt to overlook his
extreme sincerity and naturalism in the first
stages of his career.

When the statue was completed in 1504, Botti-
celli wanted to put it in the Loggia dei Lanzi;
others argued for the Duomo itself. In the end,
however, it was decided that the *David* should
be placed in front of the Palazzo Vecchio. Get-

ting him there was no easy task. First the walls of the Opera del Duomo had to be knocked down. The David 'went very slowly', Luca Landucci observed in his diary, 'being bound in an erect position and suspended so that it did not touch the ground with its feet'. The move took four days, and required forty men.

For almost four centuries, then, the *David* led a relatively peaceful life in the Piazza, except for a bad day in 1527 when a riot erupted and his left arm was broken. The incident testifies, once again, to the odd fact that heavy things can be exceptionally frail. Bad weather took its toll as well, and near the middle of the nineteenth century, as Italy was being unified and Florence was preparing for its brief moment of glory as its capital, art historians, restorers and politicians started lobbying for the necessity of finding the *David* a new home. In 1852, a commission convened to report 'on the dangers threatening the *David* and on the systems to be adopted to avoid its crumbling to the ground' voted unanimously to relocate the statue, but failed to agree on a place. The Loggia of the old market was proposed, as were the Loggia dei Lanzi (again) and the Loggia degli Uffizi, but for reasons ranging from lack of light to the fear that the statue would be subjected to the 'ravages of the lower classes', all three were rejected; so were the Medici chapel and the Bargello. Finally, in the late 1860s, another commission concluded that the only real means of providing 'the most stupendous statue of the modern age' with a place of 'refuge' was to build a temple for that exclusive purpose. This 'tribune' would be designed by the architect Antonio di Fabris as an annex to the Accademia di Belle Arti; remembering what had happened in 1504, the commission thought it prudent to move the statue to the site before construction began, so that no walls would have to be broken down.

The move was planned carefully. First, in the summer of 1873, workmen laid a railroad track across the Piazza della Signoria. The track turned right on to Via de Calzaiuoli, rounded the Duomo and made a sharp left on to Via del Cocomero (Watermelon Street, later changed to Via Ricasoli) before reaching its terminus at the Accademia. Once the track was completed, the *David* was hoisted from his pedestal and lowered into a sort of tramcar, the wooden scaffolding of which held him aloft so that his feet did not touch the ground. Finally, on 30 July, he began the journey to his new home – a journey that would last seven days, though the distance involved could be covered on foot in ten or fifteen minutes. In one of the few illustrations to be made of the move, a print published in *Nuova Illustrazione Universale* of January 1874, only the upper half of the *David*'s torso is visible above the wooden walls of the cart. His famous posture – head turned, eyes glancing hesitantly over the left shoulder – takes on new pathos in this image, as if what he is regarding with such worry is actually the gradual disappearance of the only home he has ever known.

Not everyone was happy about the move. 'Michelangelo's *David* in Piazza della Signoria is no more!!' an unnamed journalist lamented in the *Giornale Artistico* of 1 August, 1873. 'It's been embalmed and seen in a new contraption of wood and iron on its way to its burial in the Cemetery of Art vulgarly called the Accademia di Belle Arti.' A cartoon from the same period shows the *David* bending down and leaning out of his crate in order to argue with the foppish, behatted men who have presumably orchestrated his removal. A letter written to the Minister of Public Education complained of the 'degrading' cart in which the *David* was enclosed – as if the rain and wind slowly eating away at his marble body were not, in a literal sense, far more degrading. And though the rhetoric died down once the *David* was safely ensconced at the *Accademia*, a lingering annoyance at the gap left in the piazza's statuary remained, leading in 1910 (things move slowly in Florence) to the erection of the marble copy that today many tourists blithely confuse with the real thing.

Those who are more astute, of course, brave the long lines outside the Accademia in order to see *David* in his authentic and inimitable glory. Living as he does now in a tribune, one might expect him to have taken on an expression of arrogance, yet in fact – and despite the change of circumstance – his look of vulnerability seems only to have intensified over the years. Perhaps this is due to old age, a lingering ache in his left arm, or in the second toe of his left foot, which a vandal broke in 1991. To invent such a motive, I know, is to assume that the statue has an identity distinct from that of the Biblical figure it represents, or even the marble from which it was hewn; indeed, it is to assume that the statue has a consciousness. And what might such a consciousness – at once freighted and fragile – possibly resemble? What kind of memory would stone possess? We can only imagine.

Like most people, I first went to Florence for its art. That initial visit, in 1982, lasted four days and amounted to an almost complete submersion in the city's artistic heritage, a giddy alternation between heat and cool, sun-parched piazzas and churches so dark it took minutes for my eyes to adjust to them. By the time the four days were over, I had seen pretty much everything my art history professor had told me to see; I had squinted up at dozens of frescoes and altarpieces, and spent hours in the long corridors of the Uffizi; I had climbed the steep paths of the Boboli Gardens, and the operatic staircase (designed by Michelangelo) that leads to the Laurentian Library, and the spiral staircase that leads to the roof of the

Duomo. And how did I feel? Irritable, impatient, inadequate. Stendhal's Syndrome: so completely did Florence's superabundance of marvels throw off my equilibrium that at the end of my time there I decided to cut my summer vacation short and fly back to Palo Alto, drawn by a longing for those banal American things through which I hoped to restore some sense of who I was.

Living in Florence, of course, is an entirely different matter; then you almost never go to look at the art, unless a friend or relative happens to be visiting. One does not easily envision Ouida and Janet Ross and the other Anglo-Florentines making regular jaunts to the Pitti Palace; they were too busy squabbling and gossiping. By the same token, the contemporary foreigner's life in Florence, though constantly impinged upon by a persistent if only half-articulate consciousness of art's proximity, remains curiously remote from, one might even say immune to, the very patrimony that drew him in the first place. Not that the art disappears for him; it simply remains at the periphery of his imagination, awaiting the day when some unspecified incentive – the right weather, the absence of a line – induces him to make a spontaneous visit to Santa Maria del Carmine, or San Marco, or the Palazzo Medici-Riccardi . . .

What he forgets, of course, is that works of art are not immortal. Nor are they immune to catastrophes, both human and natural. In 1993, a bomb ripped through part of the Uffizi. The April before, in Florence to look for an apartment, we had stayed at the Pensione Quisisana and Ponte Vecchio, where parts of *A Room with a View* were filmed. This was a very old-fashioned pension, located on the upper floors of a *palazzo* that gives on to the Arno, a few doors down from the Uffizi. There was a dilapidated, if somewhat grand, entrance hall in which an old woman, presumably the mother or grandmother of the owner, could usually be seen, paying little attention to the television, which was always on. To reach our room, we had to traverse several short staircases (going both up and down), three corridors of varying width, and a *salone* with a white floor and a piano; as Forster noted in his 1958 afterword to *A Room with a View*, after the war the houses along that part of the Lungarno were 'renumbered and remodelled and, as it were, remelted', some of the façades extended and others shrunk so that it became 'impossible to decide which room was romantic half a century ago'. I remember that we went to a recital in the church of Santo Stefano by the Russian pianist Bella Davidovich, and then ran into her the next morning at breakfast; she too was staying at the Quisisana and Ponte Vecchio, and when we congratulated her, she removed the glove from her right hand to shake ours: a reminder that until not very long ago, most women wore gloves.

Anyway, it rained a lot on that visit. (Pino Oriolo, among others, joked about the fact that the famously glorious Tuscan spring is often no more than a succession of drenched afternoons.) We found an apartment, then flew home, with the intention of returning at the beginning of July. On the evening of 27 May, back in the States, I turned on the television news and learned that a car bomb had exploded outside the Uffizi, destroying three paintings, damaging thirty other works, and causing grave injury to the museum and to many of the buildings around it, including the one that housed the Quisisana and Ponte Vecchio. The pensione was closed, and has never reopened.

During the first months we lived in Florence – the late summer and fall of 1993 – we would often walk to the end of the Chiasso dei Baroncelli in order to observe, through a gnarled barrier of scaffolding affixed with red and white tape, the piles of rubble, metal and plastic that were the bomb's legacy. Down streets like these Lucy Honeychurch had gotten lost with Miss Lavish; now they were gutted quarries, reminiscent of those through which Michelangelo wandered. The devastation was so intense as to bring to mind photographs of the Lungarno and the Via Por Santa Maria after they were bombed by the Germans in the summer of 1945 – and yet on that occasion, at least, no great art had been destroyed. Starting in 1940, the Fascist government, with alarming foresight, had begun taking protective measures in the event that war should break out, padding some statues and removing others, along with the bronze baptistry doors, to a concrete shelter in the Boboli Gardens. At the Accademia, the Michelangelos were enclosed within brick silos. Many of the city's paintings were taken out of Florence altogether, to be housed at some of the grander villas in the countryside, among them Montagnana, Poppiano and the Castello Montegufoni, which was owned by Osbert Sitwell's father, Sir George Sitwell. In *Laughter in the Next Room*, the fourth volume of his memoir *Left Hand, Right Hand!*, Sitwell explains that Montegufoni was chosen

because it is situated in a remote district, but, still more, because the doors and windows of the chief rooms were big enough to allow the largest pictures to be carried in and out without risk of damage . . . here, very near what was to become for some days one of the most fiercely contested portions of the front line, was gathered together the rarest of all house-parties . . . among the very first arrivals, on the 18th of November [1942], were Uccello's *Battle of San Romano*, the Cimabue *Virgin Enthroned*, the great *Madonna* of Giotto, and Botticelli's *Primavera*.

For the grand sum of seventeen lire a day, Guido Masti, Sir George Sitwell's retainer, was

given the task of protecting works of art va-
lued at the time at three hundred and twenty
million dollars. Yet he was far from alone in
the castle. In 1943 Cesare Fasola, then curator
of the Uffizi, reputedly walked across the battle lines to Montegufoni, where he took up a
protective stance among the paintings he
loved. More surrealistically, as many as two
thousand refugees 'swarmed into the cellars
and dungeons from towns as far away as
Empoli and Castel Fiorentino: for the old
reputation of Montegufoni as a stronghold
had revived in the popular mind'.

There were, then, for some ten or fourteen days,
these two populations: the huddled crowds of
homeless and terrified souls in the darkness
below, where, at any rate, it was comparatively
safe, and on the ground floor above, in grave
danger, hundreds of world-famous pictures,
piled against the sides of the walls, in the lofty
painted rooms and halls. . . . Next, the Germans
arrived, occupied the Castello, and turned out
the refugees. They lived in the rooms above, and
often threatened to destroy the pictures, but
Professor Fasola and Guido Masti continued

somehow to preserve them. When the German General, on entering the Castle, uttered menacing words about these great canvases being in his way and that they should be burnt, Guido said to him, as only an Italian, with the natural imaginative rhetoric of his race, could say:

'These pictures belong not to one nation, but are the possession of the world.'

Remarkably, almost none of the works housed at Montegufoni were damaged; an exception was a circular Ghirlandaio that the Germans had used as a tabletop, and that was consequently stained with wine, food and coffee, and scarred by knives.

In his memoir *The Art of Adventure*, Eric Linklater later recalled arriving at Montegufoni with the BBC war correspondent Wynford Vaughan-Thomas, not long after the Germans had fled. 'Some refugees had been sleeping in the castello,' he wrote; '. . . cheerfully perceiving our excitement, they were making sounds of lively approval, and a couple of men began noisily to open the shutters . . . Vaughan-Thomas shouted, "Uccello!"'

I, in the same instant, cried, 'Giotto!' For a moment we stood there, quite still, held in the double grip of amazement and delight . . . We went nearer, and the refugees came round us and proudly exclaimed, '*E vero, è vero! Uccello! Giotto! Molto bello, molto antico!*' . . . Then I heard a sudden clamour of voices, a yell of shrill delight, and Vaughan-Thomas shouting 'Botti-celli!' as if he were a fox-hunter view-hallooing on a hill. I ran to see what they had found, and came to a halt before the *Primavera*.

For foreigners living in Italy, the years leading up to the war had been difficult ones to endure. As a consequence of Mussolini's rise to power and the invasion of Abyssinia, an unsuspected strain of intolerance mingled with nationalism had begun to reveal itself in the Italians, of whom the novelist Sybille Bedford – a teenager in Italy at the time – made this acute observation:

When their rules are too bad, they duck; retreat into personal relations, family relations – there you'll find riches of good behaviour, devotion *and* honour as well as endurance and courage.

Out in politics they are opportunists and show-offs, clever when they ought to be straightforward, rhetorical when they ought to go home and think, and they haven't learned how to compromise without treachery.

There was certainly little compromise under Mussolini. Among other draconian reforms introduced by *Il Duce*, foreign words were expunged from the national vocabulary. '*Autista* replaced chauffeur,' Acton remembered, '*albergo* hotel, and half the hotels in Italy had to be re-baptized in Fascist style, all the Eden Parks and Eden Palaces . . . besides the countless Albions, Bristols, and Britannias . . .' An Italian 'His Master's Voice' ('La Voice del Padrone') catalogue from the period advertises recordings by 'Wladimiro Horowitz' and 'Sergio Rachmaninoff', as well as compositions by 'Luigi Beethoven', 'Wolfango Mozart' and 'Francesco Schubert'. Predictably, such xenophobia found its easiest target in Florence, with its 'English Tea Rooms' and 'Old England' shops. Now the walls of buildings were 'scrawled all over with slogans which were meant to remind us that "*La Guerra è bella*"

David Leavitt

(War is beautiful),' while the artificial inflation of the *lira* halved the incomes of old English-women already living hand-to-mouth. Earlier, Acton had been impressed by the 'super lounge-lizards' cruising Via Tornabuoni, 'all their goods in the shop window, [spilling] on to the pavement to inspect each passing ankle and compare notes in voices loud enough to be overheard'. Now these 'unemployed Narcissi' were taking as avidly to the Blackshirt uniform as they had previously to buttonholes, brillian-tine and spats. Foreigners previously cultivated were *persone non grate*. Even Acton's mother, Hortense, was taken into custody one after-noon, under the pretense that there was a problem with her passport. For three days and nights the elderly Mrs Acton, 'in a flimsy summer dress without even a toothbrush', was 'immured among prostitutes and others of ill-repute . . .'

No message reached her from outside except an insolent letter from a Fascist female, wife of an art critic, telling her she had only got what she deserved, she might have been treated much worse, with the slogan '*Il Duce ha sempre ragi-*

one' ('The Leader is always right') appended to her florid signature. When my mother's maid telephoned a powerful friend for help, he snapped back at her: 'Don't you realize that we are at war and that Mrs Acton is an enemy alien?' That distinguished official had been a frequent guest in our house for a quarter of a century.

As a coda to this story, James Lord notes a detail that Acton, for the sake of *bella figura*, left out: in fact, the problem with Hortense Acton's passport was not an invention; she had altered 'the date of her birth to make herself appear a decade younger. Why she should have cared what customs officials and frontier police knew her age to be is a mystery, but a very significant clue must be looked for in the vanity and arrogance of the lady in question. Tampering with a passport, even for such a frivolous reason, may be considered a serious matter . . .'

In the event, as soon as she got out of jail, Mrs Acton left for Switzerland.

At last war broke out; by then all but the most entrenched colonists had, quite sensibly, fled Italy, though a few refused to abandon their houses, most notably the Jewish Bernard Berenson, who eventually had to go into hiding in the countryside. In his autobiographical film *Tea with Mussolini*, the director Franco Zeffirelli portrays a group of elderly English ladies – the sort for whom the adjective 'indomitable' is inevitably trotted out – who stick it out in Florence after war is declared and are consequently sent by the military to a makeshift prison in the hill town of San Gimignano. The film's climactic sequence, in which Judi Dench, Maggie Smith and Joan Plowright quite literally interpose themselves between the village's famous medieval towers and the Germans who intend to bomb them – thus saving art from history – makes for a camp spectacle that recalls some of the graver excesses committed by Zeffirelli in his career as an opera director; yet as a fantasy, it also highlights the intensity of the foreign community's devotion to the country they had adopted – and that they believed had adopted them.

In the end, the worst loss was that of the bridges that crossed the Arno, some of them hundreds of years old, and all of them, with the exception of the Ponte Vecchio, blown up by the Germans on 4 August 1944. Earlier the Swiss Consul, Karl Steinhauslin (after whom a Florentine bank is now named), had pleaded that the statues of the *Four Seasons* on the Ponte Santa Trinità be spared; they were not. After the liberation, divers scoured the bottom of the Arno for the statues, even as members of the all black American 387th Engineer Battalion set to work building temporary Bailey bridges of wood and steel in order to reconnect the two halves of the severed city. Eventually all four seasons were found, with the exception of spring's head, at which point, Mary McCarthy recounts in *The Stones of Florence*, a rumor began circulating that 'an American Negro soldier had been seen carrying it away during the fighting and confusion'. Posters went up all over the city, featuring a photograph of the statue, asking 'HAVE YOU SEEN THIS WOMAN?' and offering a three-thousand-dollar reward for her safe return. But the head failed to reappear, and in 1958, after a precise replica of the bridge was built using precise replicas of sixteenth-century tools, the authorities had no choice but to return a head-less spring to her old position on the northeast corner. (Only three years later, during work on the Ponte Vecchio, did the head turn up; it had not, as rumor claimed, been smuggled off to Harlem, or New Zealand, or buried in the Boboli Gardens, but had been at the bottom of the river all along.)

Today, although all the bridges that the Germans destroyed have been rebuilt, not all the Bailey bridges have been taken down; indeed, there is one near Galluzzo, on the outskirts of Florence, that we cross every time we leave to go to the country. Its wooden boards make a racket when the wheels of the car pass over them; we feel, for a few seconds, a worrisome vibration . . . and then we're on solid ground again. Every time this happens I think, for a moment, of the libera-tion I wasn't alive to witness, its much-her-alded scenes – American soldiers giving chewing gum to children – as well as those that remain unnarrated: the black members of the 387th Engineering Batallion, prohibited from actually fighting because of their race, and now going quietly about the unglamorous job of making the city whole again. Little is recalled of them, yet they did as much to save Florence as any foreigner ever has, as much as Berenson, or Henry James, or Zeffirelli's histrionic old Englishwomen. May their story, in all its amplitude, someday be told.

A river city, by its very nature, is a double city, and in this regard Florence is a cousin to Paris, Rome and Budapest; that is to say, in Florence, there are not so much two equal sides as a principal side and an 'other' side: just as Rome has Trastevere, Paris its *rive gauche* and Buda its Pest, Florence has the *Oltr'arno* – literally 'across the Arno' – a poorer zone with smaller houses, wandered by writers and drug addicts, butting up against the countryside. *Oltr'arno*'s heart is Piazza Santo Spirito, which, with its used-record shops and student bars, resembles more than any other part of Florence the Latin Quarter of Paris, despite the comparative remoteness of the university, which is to be found on the principal side of the Arno, the unnamed side, not far from Piazza Santissima Annunziata. Here, one Sunday a month, organic farmers from the Mugello and Chianti, many of them ex-hippies who passed their youth in these bars, gather to stage a market at which they sell honey and beeswax candles, homemade jam, whole-grain bread, clothes and leather goods, as well as flavorful, if not very pretty, vegetables. In contrast to the Duomo and Santa Croce, the severe façades of which were done up during Florence's brief period as a capital, the church of Santo Spirito has a stark, unadorned front that suggests the asceticism of earlier centuries. In 1980, an artist's co-operative headed by Mario Mariotti decided to redress this oversight by projecting on to Santo Spirito all manner of designs for a possible new façade; these included a fried egg (Gianni Melotti), a record album showing Nipper, emblem of 'His Master's Voice' (Gesù Moctezuma), wrapping paper (Christo, of course), and, most sportively, the interior of the church projected on to its exterior (Marianna Gagliardi).

Now as then, young foreigners love *Oltr'arno*. Even the stuffy Henry James, visiting Florence in his youth, stayed near the Ponte Vecchio on the *Oltr'arno* side. 'My room at the inn looked out on the river and was flooded all day with sunshine,' he wrote.

There was an absurd orange-coloured paper on the walls; the Arno, of a hue not altogether different, flowed beneath; and on the other side of it rose a line of sallow houses, of extreme antiquity, bulging and protruding over the stream. (I seem to speak of their fronts; but what I saw was their shabby backs, which were exposed to the cheerful flicker of the river, while the fronts stood for ever in the deep damp shadow of a narrow medieval street.)

All this 'brightness and yellowness' was for James 'a part of that indefinably charming colour which Florence always seems to wear as you look up and down at it from the river, and from the bridges and quays'. He writes of the Arno's 'silvered yellow', just as Acton describes its water as being 'a mellow yellow in the evening light; were it a little less muddy, it would pass for Orvieto wine'. Pictures from as late as the end of the nineteenth century show children and young men fishing in the river, or diving off the bridges to swim. All long gone: today, though canoes and skiffs ply its waters, no one would dare dive into the Arno; nor would a health-conscious person want to eat a fish caught in it. During the hottest part of the summer, the water level drops, the river becomes stagnant, sludge-green (I have never seen it yellow) and musky. Mice and rats scurry in the shallows and bats fly overhead in the muggy air. ('*Guarda*, it is so romantic, with the full moon and the *topi* swimming in the river!' waxes our friend from Cozensa, the one who likes to dress as Cardinal Richelieu.) In the winter, on the other hand, when the rains come, the Arno is cappuccino-colored; it rushes violently, carrying oak and chestnut branches downstream from its source in the Mugello.

Flood is a constant threat. Although the Arno has overflowed its banks on dozens of occasions over the centuries, the worst floods have tended to take place at hundred-year intervals, usually in years with double or even triple digits: 1333, 1466, 1557, 1844, 1966. (The superstitious Florentine looks forward to another disastrous *alluvione* in 2055 or 2077.) These floods can start up with little or no warning. The flood of 4 November 1966 started off the night before as a heavy rain, and only began to threaten in the early hours of the morning. By two a.m., the owners of some of the jewelry stores on the Ponte Vecchio, having been alerted by the night watchman on the bridge, were hurrying to their shops to rescue what they could of their stock. There was some worry that the ancient bridge itself might collapse, though it had survived other floods as well as the war. One shopkeeper later recalled seeing a Fiat 1100 butting at the window of his store.

More than 15,000 cars were destroyed during the flood. Perhaps because the average Florentine, in 1966, took great pride in owning a car – even a tiny, pumpkin-colored Fiat 500 – television footage shot in the immediate aftermath of the disaster has a curiously obsessive quality, as it bypasses churches and monuments to move from car to car to car: upturned, floating, muddrenched, oil-drenched. There is something funereal about this photographic record, the pictures of destroyed cars recalling the snapshots of the dead that Italians place on gravestones.

Less attention was paid to injured art, though in fact this was the graver consequence, since cars are replaceable and Renaissance frescoes are not. A catalogue prepared by UNESCO offers numbing evidence of just how much was damaged: 321 paintings on wood, 413 on canvas, 11 fresco cycles, 70 individual frescoes (a total of around 3,000 square meters of fresco), 14 sculptural groups, 144 individual sculptures (including several by Michelangelo), 22 of them in wood: in all, close to a thousand works of major historical importance. The rushing waters, which reached a height of nearly six meters inside the Duomo, tore the bronze doors off the Baptistry. Once these had subsided, a slimy, corrosive mixture of heating oil and mud, in places as much as four feet deep, remained in their wake; in this *melma* several of Ghiberti's bronze panels were found steeping the next day.

Sometimes the *melma*'s effects could be weirdly dramatic. As Guido Gerosa wrote, in the aftermath of the flood Donatello's statue of the Magdalen 'was transmuted into a a mask of mud . . . The monstrous smears of diesel fuel that furrowed her long loose hair seemed paradoxically to intensify her look of dramatic desperation.' The same could not be said of Cimabue's famous Crucifix at Santa Croce, which was found broken into rubble. Nor were paintings the only precious things to suffer. A photograph taken at the Teatro Comunale shows a Steinway piano swollen from submersion and caked in mud. At the Biblioteca Nazionale, more than 700,000 rare books and manuscripts, as well as the newspaper and magazine collection, all of which had been stored in a basement, were waterlogged. On this point in particular, much criticism was leveled at the Florentine authorities, whose decision not merely to construct the library along the river banks (an absurdly vulnerable position) but to house rarities in its basement now provoked bewilderment and outrage both among Italians and foreigners. For the first time since the days when Ruskin had protested the construction of an omnibus stand in front of the bell tower, James's 'Florentine question' – the question of whether the Florentines could be trusted with their own patrimony – revived noisily. In London, Sir Ashley Clarke quickly established the Italian Art and Archives Rescue Fund, under the aegis of which the restorer Nicolai Rubinstein and the art historian John

Pope-Hennessy were sent to Florence to assess the damage. Later, Pope-Hennessy would recall finding Donatello's *Annunziazione dei Cavalcanti*, in the nave of Santa Croce, 'soaked with oil to the level of the Virgin's knees'.

In addition to Santa Croce, the cloisters of Santa Maria Novella and the Ognissanti had been submerged to a level of four meters. There had been damage at the Casa Buonarroti and the Museo Horne, as well as the Museum of the History of Science, the Archaeological Museum, the Bargello and in the restoration workshops on the ground floor of the Uffizi.

Even as Italian television continued to focus compulsively on wrecked cars, both within Italy and abroad a grassroots rescue movement was beginning to take shape. The men and women, most of them young, who came to Florence by the thousands to volunteer in the digging out would later be dubbed the *angeli del fango*, or 'mud angels'. (Their number included the pianist Sviatoslov Richter.) Senator Edward Kennedy, in Geneva when the flood occurred, recalled flying into Florence for the day. Arriving at the Biblioteca around five in the afternoon, he discovered masses of students up to their waists in water, working by candlelight. 'They had formed a line to pass along the books,' he wrote, 'so that they could be retrieved from the water and then handed on to a safer area to have preservatives put on them.'

Everywhere I looked in the great main reading room, there were hundreds and hundreds of young people who had all gathered to help.

It was as if they knew that this flooding of the library was putting their souls at risk. I found it incredibly inspiring to see this younger generation all united in this vital effort . . . I was still shivering as I boarded the plane that took me back to Geneva, but I couldn't stop thinking of the impressive solemnity of that scene – of all those students, oblivious to the biting cold and the muddy water, quietly concentrating on saving books in the flickering candlelight. I will never forget it.

In 1996, the thirtieth anniversary of the flood, Italy's Legambiente, using the Internet as a tool, launched an international effort to track down the mud angels and invite them to return to Florence. Testimony was solicited, much of it humbling. Marika Spence Sales, then a student at McGill University in Montreal, wrote that after the flood, she and fourteen fellow students had traveled to Florence on their own initiative. As soon as they arrived they were sent to the Biblioteca Nazionale. 'We worked in a chain system for 7–8 hours a day,' she writes, 'to pad the flooded books out with absorbent paper. We stayed at the National Library for three months. We were given food and lodging and at lunchtime ate a hot meal in the city council canteen. It was very cold in the Library. My university sent us parcels containing wellington boots and warm clothing . . . Our families sent us unperishable food instead, like powdered milk and tinned meals.'

Spence Sales met her future husband while she was in Florence, and stayed on in Italy. So did Susan Glasspool, who had just arrived from England to study at the Academy of Fine Arts when the flood hit. 'I was staying at Trespiano, outside Florence,' she recalled, 'and on the morning of the flood, a landslide had blocked the road close by the house. We didn't realise that there had been a flood and thought that the bad weather was the cause of the lack of electricity, phone and water. My landlady somehow heard that something serious had happened in Florence and asked me if I could drive her down to see if her relations were in need of any help.'

Once they arrived, they discovered a city all but crippled; in particular, Glasspool was amazed that the Ponte Vecchio, 'which was completely jammed up with tree trunks', was still standing. She was quickly put to work 'cleaning the mud out of the cellars at the University in Piazza Brunelleschi, or helping to clear out the Uffizi Archives, the Academy or other parts of the University'. John Schofield, who traveled to Florence from London at his own expense after the flood, worked first at the Museo dell'Opera del Duomo and then in the Limonaia of the Boboli Gardens, which had been 'converted for the controlled drying of shelf upon shelf of damaged pictures'. Under the supervision of the art historian Ugo Baldini, Schofield, who would go on to make a career as an architectural restorer, 'learned to treat the packs of the pictures against virulent, many-coloured moulds. I progressed from carefully removing caked-on mud to the fungicidal treatment of the paint surface of all the pictures in rotation – a task which left no time even for a visit to the Uffizi!'

Generally speaking, the Florentines greeted the mud angels as warmly as they had the troops of liberating soldiers who had marched into the city after the war; some, however, saw them as little more than freeloading hippies. Amy Centers, the American producer of an online 'living guidebook' to Florence, describes a student named Mario who had been a young teenager living near Santa Croce when the flood hit. 'Florence in '66 had yet to see the hippie movement,' she writes, 'and the mass of long-haired, tattooed, pot-smoking teenagers in sandals, tie-dye and cut-offs was a shock to the local population. People from all over the world descended on the city to help, but as it turns out, charitable intentions were about all they had. With little money and no place to stay, the Italians were forced to house and feed them. Mario said that everywhere he went people were handing him bread, which he took, not wanting to appear rude. At the end of the night he'd go home to mountains of bread in his living room.'

And yet the last word must really be given to the students who, no matter how they dressed and how much bread they ate, came to Florence for only one reason: to help. In 1966, Catherine Williams of Bradenton, Florida, was taking her junior year abroad, studying at Florida State University's Florence campus, which had just opened. The day before the flood, she wrote, had been 'wet and miserable – I'd spent the day in Fiesole with a friend and came back in the rain to the Hotel. The next morning we heard that the Arno had flooded – the flood came up to our street [Via Aprile] and stopped – no lights, no water. We set out to explore and were met with cars wrapped around poles, mud caked on buildings – mud, mud everywhere.'

Over the next few days, Williams learned to brush her teeth with bubbly water. She and her fellow students 'stood in line for water from the military tanks and spent the days in the basement of the library', taking part in the famous human chain that Senator Kennedy memorialized. 'I spent my twentieth birthday at Florence in flood,' she wrote upon learning of the Legambiente's reunion. 'I can think of no more fitting place to be for my fiftieth.'

CHAPTER FIVE

When Mark and I went to live in Florence in 1993, a friend of ours suggested that I should write a profile of the recently knighted (and now very old) Sir Harold Acton for *The New Yorker*. I put her off, just as I put off the various contacts who offered to introduce me to Sir Harold, and in February of the next year, he died. Opportunity missed – and entirely through my own resistance. And yet, if truth be told, I've never regretted that lost chance, just as I've never regretted not going to visit Hugh Honour and John Fleming, famed art historians in residence near Lucca, to whom a hundred friends offered to introduce us; or not accepting the invitation of Gil

Cohen and Paul Gervais, a rich American couple known behind their backs (homosexual circles are bitchy) as 'Pill and Gil', to spend a weekend in their villa, also near Lucca; or never getting a private tour of the palaces of the various Corsinis and Ruccelais and Frescobaldis, the princesses and barons and *marchesi*, whom it has been the ambition since time immemorial, or at least since Henry James, of American expatriates to cultivate . . . The fact is, neither Mark nor I has ever been very interested in meeting famous or titled people simply because they were famous or titled. In this regard we differed drastically from the vast majority of the foreigners who had settled in Florence, and for whom the totting down of noteworthy names under the categories 'met', 'dined with', 'received letters from', 'was invited to drinks by' and 'slept with' provided a crucial and consuming activity – an antidote to long winter nights and stifling summer afternoons. Acton was emblematic of this tendency; although, by his old age, he had become an icon in his own right (if a pinchbeck one), in his salad days he was merely another young seeker after the anoint-

ing kiss of celebrity, planning his life, it sometimes seemed, around the objective of having
something to write memoirs about when he
was older. 'Society', the blandishments of the
Emerald Cunards and Sybil Colefaxes of the
world, entranced him, and to guarantee its
approbation, he granted himself a fatal exemp-
tion from the rule of rigor and truthfulness. No
writer can afford to be so polite, if he hopes to
be remembered as anything other than a 'character'.

I grew up in California, in a university town
ruled by an etiquette far less daunting than
that which obtained in Acton's Florence, and
which in any case my mother, never one to
suffer fools gladly, flouted at every opportunity. American to the core, as well as slightly
famous in my own right, I arrived in Florence
not knowing who Principessa Giorgiana Corsini was, much less worrying how to wangle a
lunch invitation out of her. Mark was the same
way; we thought of ourselves as sons of Forster, and for Forster, 'society' had never been
the bailiwick that it was for Acton or James.
Instead it was the Florence of the Florentines
that we longed to know, the streets and the

bars and the 'authentic' restaurants. Who cared about being invited to tea at La Pietra? What was the point, anyway, of having 'tea' when one could have a cappuccino? And so we never went, never ate the famously thin sandwiches, or received the tour of the gardens that Acton himself still sometimes gave. Others did; until his death visitors with connections, friends of friends, descended on La Pietra, if for no other reason than so that they could later say they had had tea there, seen both the villa and its legendary occupant, 'preserved – or imprisoned – within it', as James Lord wrote, 'like some gorgeous prehistoric lepidopteran in a gem of amber'. Acton's own fear was that he would be remembered only for the villa, not for his books, yet as Lord points out, the names of collectors – of owners – do not have the same staying power, in our memory, as those of artists. And that is the sad irony, that in the long run, Acton will probably be remembered neither for his writing nor for his villa; instead he will be remembered, if he is remembered, as the model for Anthony Blanche in *Brideshead Revisited*; the very 'smear' he most hoped to erase.

That said, in the early years of our Florentine idyll, we did touch on two of the surviving
relics of Anglo-Florentine society, both of
whom have since died. The first of these was
Joan Haslip. Although she had lived in Florence since her girlhood, like many of the
Anglo-Florentines, Haslip had never learned
to speak Italian. Her mother, who was half-
Austrian and half-Slav, had brought her and
her sister, Lallie, there after the death of their
English father, George Ernest Haslip. (Lallie
went on to marry Pifi Gomez, the mayor of
Florence under *Il Duce*.)

We met her only once, when we were invited
on an hour's notice to a luncheon at the five-
star Hotel Helvetia-Bristol hosted by Fausto
Calderai – a furniture expert and cog in
Florentine society. The author of numerous
biographies, among them lives of Marie An-
toinette, Madame Du Barry, Lucrezia Borgia,
Catherine the Great, Elizabeth of Austria (*The
Lonely Empress*) and Lady Hester Stanhope,
she was now in her early eighties. Decidedly
poor – like most Anglo-Florentines, she had
never bought property – she lived simply in a
small house on the property of her friend

David Leavitt

Costanza Ricasoli-Romanelli, attended by servants as old as she was, and surrounded by family furniture for which she was hoping to find a buyer who would let her continue to use it until her death.

Over drinks, Fausto asked her how she was feeling. 'I'm terrible,' she said. 'My best friends are both dying.' (She meant Acton – who left her nothing in his will – and John Pope-Hennessy). Haslip herself was arthritic and close to blind, yet when Principessa Corsini, another guest at the lunch, asked if she wouldn't do better with a wheelchair, she pushed aside the suggestion with the same gesture she used to keep her hair aloft – no matter that Florence was full of history-besotted young men who would have enjoyed nothing better than taking her around town. After all, she was still a brilliant *raconteuse*, full of secrets about royalty and smuggled emeralds. Her coquettish wit suggested what Via Tornabuoni must have been like during her youth – those days when, in Acton's words, the street was 'aureoled with Ouida-esque romance', and when she had written a breathless novel about Florence, *Grandfather's Steps* (dedicated to Lallie), as well as a poem, *Peonies and Magnolias*, published in a limited edition by Centaur Booklets, and of which the following lines are exemplary:

> Luigi, Gianni, Mario
> In pink and lilac shirts.
> They are the vital topics,
> The season's fav'rite flirts.

When Pope-Hennessy's friend Michael Mallon, to whom Haslip willed her library, asked if she might ever consider writing fiction again, she said there was no point: no one was interested in reading novels about the upper classes any more.

She had not given up biography, however. At the Helvetia-Bristol someone (perhaps the French consul) inquired if she was at work on something new. 'I'm doing Napoleon's sisters,' she answered, 'and they're behaving *exactly* like the royal princesses.' (This was before one royal princess died in a car crash and the other became a spokeswoman for Weight Watchers.)

Later, when Fausto told her (inaccurately)

that Mark was Margaret Mitchell's grandson, she became exuberant. 'It's my favorite film,' she said. 'Tell me, are you still living off it?'

As lunch ended, she made a show of telling Fausto she'd brought the wrong purse, the one without the money: could he arrange a taxi for her?

Haslip's other best friend, Sir John Wyndham Pope-Hennessy (fondly known as 'the Pope'), died on Halloween of that year, which seemed weirdly apposite, given his legendary chilliness; after all, this was a man who had recalled a trip to the morgue to identify the body of his brother James – beaten to death by hustlers in a Ladbroke Grove maisonette (another arrow in your side, Labouchère!) – with the following words: 'I was appalled by the dissolute, almost evil expression of his face. It was as though one were participating in a Jacobean tragedy.'

Although he had spent his summers in the city for forty years, Pope-Hennessy was a relative newcomer to the residential colony in Florence, having settled there only in 1986. (Before that he had lived in New York, where he served as Consultative Chairman in the Department of European Paintings at the Met, and before that in London, where he was director of the Victoria and Albert Museum, then of the British Museum.) In Florence he rented a vast apartment in the Palazzo Canigiani on Via de' Bardi, famous from George Eliot's novel *Romola*. With its magnificent loggia overlooking the Arno and Fiesole, the apartment suggested the grand style, the cultured elegance, to which the Anglo-Florentines of a century earlier had accustomed themselves so quickly: at the end of the nineteenth century a castle could cost less than an antique majolica jar. There were several 'important' paintings, and much 'important' furniture, including a round porphyry and cherry-wood table that we particularly coveted. Yet the most memorable detail of the apartment was not grand at all: it was an odd little window in one of the corridors, a window that started halfway down the wall and ended at the floor, so that you could sit on the carpet and dangle your legs out.

During his years at the V & A, Pope-Hennessy had earned a reputation for severity, even brutality, yet we saw little of this side to his character on the occasions when we visited him. By then, frail and ill, he merely presided over numerous teas and lunches. At these gatherings an uncompromisingly 'English' quality prevailed, which was surprising, given his status as a self-proclaimed exile. (Michael Mallon told us that Pope-Hennessy returned to London only three times after 1986.) No matter how hot the day, hot tea – as well as polite sandwiches and cakes – was served. Like most Italian residences, the apartment had no air-conditioning, but not for the Italian reason of habit: air-conditioning is damaging to art and furniture. The guests, mostly English or American, would mill around the living room, where Rutilio Manetti's painting of *The Madonna and Child with the Infant Saint John the Baptist and Saint Catherine of Siena* hung over the fireplace, or chat in the dining room, under a view of Lake Geneva by Simon Malgo; after the Pope's death, this painting sold at Christie's for $178,500.

It was hard to recognize in our octogenerian host the ferocious advocate of 'standards' who had quarrelled so irascibly with Roy Strong, his successor at the V & A, or the critic who had once claimed that objects meant more to him than people, or even the legendary *provocateur* who had balked at Mary McCarthy's astringency (the pot calling the kettle black!). Indeed, on only one occasion did this side of his personality assert itself in our presence. We had just sat down to lunch when rather casually he mentioned that Sir Stephen Spender and his wife Natasha had been his guests the week before. Pope-Hennessy knew, of course, that Spender had sued me a few months earlier over a novel I had written. 'I suspect I'm the only person in the world who's had both Spender and Leavitt to lunch within the same week,' he said, and chuckled quietly.

Pope-Hennessy's funeral mass – like Acton, like Scott Moncrieff, like so many of the Anglo-Florentines, he was a Catholic convert – took place in a small church on Piazza Santissima Annunziata (but not *the* great church of Santissima Annunziata, where for generations Florentine families have celebrated their weddings, baptisms and confirmations; that would have been too showy). Fewer mourners turned up than we expected. Shirley Hazzard, the novelist, came up from Naples, where her

David Leavitt

husband, Francis Steegmuller, had died only a
week before. The music critic Andrew Porter
flew in from London, Everett Fahy, director of
European Paintings at the Met, from New
York. Thekla Clark, an American long resident in Florence, and soon to publish a memoir
of her friends W.H. Auden and Chester Kall-
man, drove in from Bagno a Ripoli. Not
surprisingly, several scions of the Florentine
aristocracy were in attendance, as were several
young (and not so young) exemplars of that
species of Italian homosexual whose chief ambition seems to be to endear himself to the
titled. Eye contact was assiduously avoided; a
mass was intoned; few words were said.

Afterwards, at Robiglio, a good *pasticerria*
not far from the modest church, the splendors of
Florence could not have seemed more distant,
even though the Duomo was rising up as start-
lingly as ever at the end of Via dei Servi. Talk of
urban difficulties – smog, traffic, tourists –
filtered through the coffee-smelling atmosphere
along with cigarette smoke and the chorus, 'It's
the end of an era.' For the death of the Pope had
followed in quick succession those of Acton (in
February) and of Haslip (in July).

It really was the end of an era: in the course of less than a year, the famed Anglo-Florentine colony that had flourished and waned and flourished and waned over a hundred and fifty years had lost its last three monuments.

Of course, reading over the above paragraphs, I'm struck by the degree to which, without ever intending to, I seem to have adopted the very tone of the Anglo-Florentine memoirist that earlier I saw fit to decry. When describing Pope-Hennessy's funeral, for instance, which names have I given? Those that you are most likely to recognize. And why, in any case, am I writing about Pope-Hennessy in the first place, when I met him only a few times, and when I could have written just as easily about any number of other people? Even today the bug of the colony, its obsession with titles and fame, is hard to evade in the Florentine fishbowl; it is so much an element of the view that it presses, as it were, through the glass, and becomes part of the viewer, too.

The key to the history of foreigners in Florence, like the key to Florence, lies in the city's provincial character; once, much happened here, but that was a long time ago, and over a century and a half, as Florence became more and more a museum, its foreign residents – many of whom started off as observers – came to be regarded, increasingly, as part of the exhibit. 'Rather than face the uncertainty of a future in England,' James Lord writes, Acton 'fled to the other side of the earth . . . And when it was too late for a grand and uncompromising apotheosis, he found himself climbing over the back wall of the villa within which he would ultimately be confined like the legendary person known as Sir Harold Acton.' For that legendary person, as for most of the members of the colony, Florence betrayed its own promise of a freedom unimaginable on other shores, the mirage of fulfillment (George Emerson's elusive 'it') retreated into the distance, and the paradise of exiles revealed itself for what it really was: the most elegant, interesting and comfortable of prisons.

NOTES FOR
FURTHER READING

For the general reader, I can recommend no
better guide to the city of Florence than
Christopher Hibbert's *Florence: The Biography of a City* (Viking, 1993). This richly
illustrated history not only provided a constant source of reference, but pointed the way
to other texts that proved to be of value, most
notably Monica Stirling's *The Fine and the
Wicked: The Life and Times of Ouida* (Gollancz, 1957) and Eric Linklater's *The Art of
Adventure* (Macmillan, 1947). Hibbert was
also the source for quotations from Walter
Savage Landor and William Holman Hunt on
the 'stinks' of Florence, Henry James on

David Leavitt

Vernon Lee, and Luca Landucci on the original moving of the *David*. Finally, a fascinating image of the second moving of the *David*, reproduced in Hibbert, provoked my research on that subject.

I began my study of the Anglo-Florentine colony by reading the only two books on the subject in English: Olive Hamilton's *Paradise of Exiles: Tuscany and the British* (André Deutsch, 1974) and *The Divine Country: The British in Tuscany 1372–1980* (André Deutsch, 1982), by the same author. I also consulted Giuliana Artom Treves' *Anglo-Fiorentini di cento anni fa* (Sansoni, 1953; reprinted 1982).

Although many novels have been set in Florence, none approaches, in my view, E.M. Forster's *A Room with a View* (1908; reprinted in the Abinger Edition, 1978) for its insightful portrait of the city's character. Other novels set in Florence to which I refer are Henry James's *The Portrait of a Lady* (1881; reprinted by Penguin, 1984), William Dean Howells' *Indian Summer* (1886; reprinted in the Library of America, 1982), D.H. Lawrence's *Aaron's Rod* (1922; reprinted by Pengin, 1976) and Francis King's *The Ant Colony* (Constable, 1988). Harold Acton's 'The Soul's Gymnasium' is from the collection *The Soul's Gymnasium and Other Stories* (Hamish Hamilton, 1982). While not directly concerned with Florence, Sybille Bedford's *Jigsaw: A Biographical Novel* (Alfred A. Knopf, 1989) offers a shrewd account of the rise of Italian fascism, worth the attention of any reader interested in this period.

Mikhail Kuzmin's 1906 *Wings* (tr. Michael Green, Ardis, 1980) provided a fascinating perspective on the Russian colony in Florence, as did the excerpts from the journals of Nazar Litrov quoted in *Tchaikovsky through Others' Eyes*, edited by Alexander Poznansky (Indiana University Press, 1999). I learned about Vladimir de Pachmann's time in Florence from Mark Mitchell's *Vladimir de Pachmann: A Life Observed* (Indiana University Press, forthcoming).

Memoirs written by or about foreigners in Florence are legion. The ones on which I drew most heavily were Harold Acton's *Memoirs of an Aesthete* (Methuen, 1948) and *More Memoirs of an Aesthete* (Hamish

David Leavitt

Hamilton, 1970), and G. Pino Orioli's *Adventures of a Bookseller* (privately printed, 1937). In Harry Brewster's *The Cosmopolites: A Nineteenth-Century Family Drama* (Michael Russell, 1994), I found Adolf von Hildebrand's remarks on Vernon Lee as well as Lisl von Herzogenberg's on Clara Schumann, while Barbara Strachey's *Remarkable Relations: The Story of the Pearsall Smith Family* (Gollancz, 1980) was the source for some of the material concerning Mary and Bernard Berenson, Maud Cruttwell and 'the Mikes'. I also read James Lord's extraordinary recollection of his friendship with Harold Acton, 'The Cost of the Villa', included in *Some Remarkable Men: Further Memoirs* (Farrar, Straus, Giroux, 1996); Francis King's *Yesterday Came Suddenly* (Constable, 1993); Jocelyn Brooke's *Private View* (James Barrie, 1954); and John Pope-Hennessy's *Learning to Look* (Heinemann, 1991). The lines from Michael Field's 'Variations on Sappho' were found in *The Penguin Book of Homosexual Verse*, edited by Stephen Coote (Penguin, 1983).

I obtained a multi-generational perspective

on the Anglo-Florentine colony by reading Janet Ross's *The Fourth Generation* (Constable, 1912), her daughter Lina Waterfield's *Castle in Italy* (Thomas Y. Crowell, 1961), and her granddaughter Kinta Beevor's *A Tuscan Childhood* (Viking, 1993). An interesting coda to my account of Anglo-Florentine feuds was a campaign staged in 1993 by Beevor and her son, Antony, to force the writer Joanna Trollope to withdraw a novel she had recently published under the pseudonym Caroline Harvey. According to the Beevors, the novel, *A Castle in Italy*, paralleled too closely the life and memoirs of Lina Waterfield. Their efforts suggest that the Anglo-Florentines' fondness for litigation and battle, as well as their tendency to regard personal history as personal property, have in no way diminished over the course of a century.

Passages on Florence by Henry James are taken from three essays in his 1909 volume *Italian Hours*, reprinted in the Library of America: 'The Autumn in Florence' (1873), 'Italy Revisited' (1877) and 'Two Old Houses and Three Young Women' (1899). The passages from John Ruskin to which James took such exception are from *Mornings in Florence: Being Simple Studies of Christian Art for English Travellers* (Orpington, 1875–77). All quotations from Walter Pater are from *Studies in the History of the Renaissance*, originally published in 1873. My edition (Senate, 1998) is based on the 1893 text, the last known to have been revised by Pater himself. Remarks by George Eliot and the Reverend John Wordsworth on Pater are quoted in Denis Donoghue's *Walter Pater: Lover of Strange Souls* (Alfred A. Knopf, 1995).

Biographies of writers, artists and politicians who lived in or visited Florence yielded a wealth of information. Among the most illuminating was Caroline Moorehead's *Iris Origo: Marchese of Val d'Orcia* (John Murray, 2000). I also consulted Frances Kiernan's *Seeing Mary Plain: A Life of Mary McCarthy* (W.W. Norton, 2000), Selena Hastings' *Evelyn Waugh: A Biography* (Sinclair-Stevenson, 1994), Frank Harris' 1916 *Oscar Wilde* (reprinted by Robinson, 1992), Richard Ellmann's *Oscar Wilde* (Hamish Hamilton, 1987), Hesketh Pearson's *Labby: The Life and Character of Henry Labouchère* (Harper, 1937), John

Mitzel's *John Horne Burns: An Appreciative Biography* (Manifest Destiny, 1974) and Miriam J. Benkowitz's *Ronald Firbank* (Alfred A. Knopf, 1969). A new biography of Firbank, by Richard Canning, is forthcoming. The Firbank novels from which I quote are *The Flower Beneath the Foot* (1923) and *Sorrow in Sunlight*, also known as *Prancing Nigger* (1924). Both are included in *Five Novels* (New Directions, 1981). All passages from Firbank's letters and diaries are quoted in Benkowitz.

Poems about the Anglo-Florentines by Osbert Sitwell come from his collection *Poems about People*, or *England Reclaimed* (Hutchinson, 1958). In addition, I quote from *Noble Essences* (Macmillan, 1950), the last volume in Sitwell's five-part memoir *Left Hand, Right Hand!*

The cookbooks cited are Giacomo Castelvetro's *The Fruits, Herbs and Vegetables of Italy: An Offering to Lucy, Countess of Bedford*, written while Castelvetro was in exile in England in the early seventeenth century (tr. Gillian Riley, Viking, 1989) and *Leaves from our Tuscan Kitchen* by Janet Ross, revised by

Michael Waterfield (Penguin, 1977). For those wanting to learn more about Tuscan cooking, I would recommend Pellegrino Artusi's classic *The Art of Eating Well* (1891), recently translated into English by Kyle M. Phillips III (Random House, 1996).

The most authoritative source on Florentine attitudes toward homosexuality is Michael Rocke's *Forbidden Friendships: Homosexuality and Male Culture in Renaissance Florence* (Oxford University Press, 1996). H. Montgomery Hyde's *The Other Love: An Historical and Contemporary Survey of Homosexuality in Britain* (Heinemann, 1970) is full of useful information on English homosexuals who fled to Florence, as well as on the Labouchère Amendment and its legal ramifications. Also valuable were Hyde's *The Cleveland Street Scandal* (Coward, McCann & Geoghegan, 1976), Timothy d'Arch Smith's *Love in Earnest* (Routledge and Keegan Paul, 1970), and Edward Prime-Stevenson's *The Intersexes*, published under the pseudonym Xavier Mayne (reprinted by Arno, 1975).

The epigraph is taken from *The Memoirs of*

John Addington Symonds, edited by Phyllis Grosskurth (Hutchinson, 1984). I quote from Symonds' *The Life of Michelangelo Buonarroti* (Modern Library, 1928) in the section on the moving of Michelangelo's *David*, for which my other principal source was *The Place for David: The Accademia, Michelangelo, The Nineteenth Century*, edited by Franca Falletti (Sillabe, 1997). For the sections on Florence during World War II and on the flood of 1966, I relied on Paolo Paoletti's *Firenze, guerra e alluvione* (Becocci, 1991) and on a number of Internet sites, most notably *www.qmfound.com/black service units in combat.htm, www.homestead.com/florence101/italyupdate.html* and *www.mega.it/allu/eng/rispts.htm*. A novel about the mud angels is Robert Hellenga's *The Sixteen Pleasures* (Soho, 1994).

I found photographs (by Massimo Listri) of the images projected by artists on to the façade of Santo Spirito in Mario Mariotti's *Piazza S. Spirito* (Alinari, 1981).

Lastly, I would be remiss if I did not recommend Mary McCarthy's *The Stones of Florence* (Harcourt Brace, 1959), one of the

few genuinely literary responses that the city
has ever generated. The book is ill-tempered
and opinionated – sometimes vexingly so; it
never fails to delight me.

A NOTE ON THE TYPE

The text of this book is set in Linotype Sabon,
named after the type founder, Jacques Sabon. It
was designed by Jan Tschichold and jointly
developed by Linotype, Monotype and Stempel, in
response to a need for a typeface to be available
in identical form for mechanical hot metal
composition and hand composition using foundry
type. Tschichold based his design for Sabon roman
on a fount engraved by Garamond, and Sabon
italic on a fount by Granjon. It was first used in
1966 and has proved an enduring modern classic.

1 MEDICI CHAPELS
2 BIB. LAURENZIANA
3 P. MEDICI RICCARDI
4 CAMPANILE DI GIOTTO
5 PIAZZA D. SIGNORIA
6 LOGGIA DEI LANZI
7 BIBLIOTECA NAZIONALE
8 PONTE VECCHIO
9 PONTE S. TRINITA

STAZIONE CENTRALE

S. MARIA

NOVELLA

VIA D. GIG

OGNISSANTI

VIA D FOSSI

PALAZZO
CORSINI

VIA D. TORNAB

FIUME

S. M. DEL
CARMINE

S. SPIRITO

V. MAGGIO

PISA

VIA D. SERRAGLI

V. ROMANA